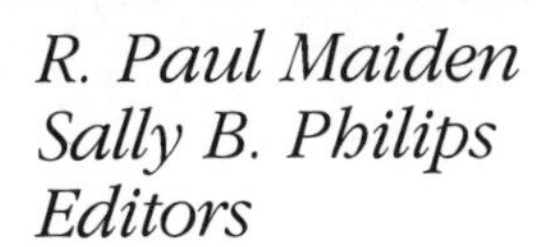
R. Paul Maiden
Sally B. Philips
Editors

Employee Assistance Programs in Higher Education

Employee Assistance Programs in Higher Education has been co-published simultaneously as *Journal of Workplace Behavioral Health*, Volume 22, Numbers 2/3, 2006/2007.

Pre-publication REVIEWS, COMMENTARIES, EVALUATIONS . . .

"A resource that WILL BE TREASURED BY BOTH NEWCOMERS AND SEASONED VETERANS. . . . Gives very practical advice for the post 9/11 EAPs of today, including how to respond to campus traumas, coaching, responding to the death of a colleague, providing management consultation, and the ever present challenge of providing services to faculty. . . . SHOULD ALSO BE INSTRUCTIVE TO THOSE ADMINISTRATORS CONSIDERING IMPLEMENTING A PROGRAM FOR THEIR SCHOOL."

Tom Ruggieri, LCSW-C
Faculty Staff Assistance Program
University of Maryland College Park

More pre-publication
REVIEWS, COMMENTARIES, EVALUATIONS . . .

"A TIMELY COLLECTION of practitioner-based articles which are SURE TO BECOME ESSENTIAL READING for EAP professionals practicing in academic settings. . . . An additional strength of the book is the inclusion of topics that go beyond standard EAP consultation to address needs related to the new business models many academic institutions are embracing. . . . ESPECIALLY USEFUL FOR PRACTITIONERS to hone their skills as well as add value to the organizations and clients they serve. I RECOMMEND THIS WELL THOUGHT-OUT EDITION for any academic EAP professional or graduate student seeking career guidance."

Nadeen Medvin, PhD, DABPS
City of Miami
Employee Assistance Program Administrator
Adjunct Professor of Human Resource Management
Organizational Behavior, and Psychometrics
University of Miami
Florida International University

"Few in the EAP field have the depth of experience of Paul Maiden and Sally Phillips of programs in both the corporate and academic world. . . . ESSENTIAL READING here for the experienced as well as the entry level professional. . . . OF SPECIAL VALUE to the Human Resource professionals who want to have an understanding of the thinking in EAPs, their problems, and methods. . . . Though written for the EAP specialist, both the person deciding whether to work in the field, or an executive deciding whether to establish a program will find great help here."

Wm. Harry Brownlee, MD (retired)
Dept. of Psychiatry
Columbia University College of Physicians and Surgeons; Founder
Brownlee Dolan Stein Association

Employee Assistance Programs in Higher Education

Employee Assistance Programs in Higher Education has been co-published simultaneously as *Journal of Workplace Behavioral Health*, Volume 22, Numbers 2/3, 2006/2007.

Monographic Separates from the *Journal of Workplace Behavioral Health*™

For additional information on these and other Haworth Press titles, including descriptions, tables of contents, reviews, and prices, use the QuickSearch catalog at http://www.HaworthPress.com.

The *Journal of Workplace Behavioral Health*™ is the successor title to *Employee Assistance Quarterly*®,* which changed title after Vol. 19, No. 4, 2004. The *Journal of Workplace Behavioral Health*™, under its new title, begins with Vol. 20, No. 1/2/3/4, 2005.

Employee Assistance Programs in Higher Education, edited by R. Paul Maiden, PhD, and Sally B. Philips, EdD (Vol. 22, No. 2/3, 2006/2007). *"A resource that will be treasured by both newcomers and seasoned veterans." (Tom Ruggieri, LCSW-C, Faculty Staff Assistance Progam, University of Maryland College Park)*

Workplace Disaster Preparedness, Response, and Management, edited by R. Paul Maiden, PhD, Rich Paul, MSW, and Christina Thompson, MSW (Vol. 21, No. 3/4, 2006). *Examination on strategies to provide crisis response services for professionals and employers responsible for planning and coordinating organizational responses to disasters.*

The Integration of Employee Assistance, Work/Life, and Wellness Services, edited by Mark Attridge, PhD, Patricia A. Herlihy, PhD, RN, and R. Paul Maiden, PhD, LCSW (Vol. 20, No. 1/2/3/4, 2005). *"A must read for anyone who is providing or purchasing employee assistance, work-life, or wellness programs." (Paul A. Courtois, MSW, Senior Auditor, Corporate Audit Services)*

Accreditation of Employee Assistance Programs,* edited by R. Paul Maiden, PhD (Vol. 19, No. 1, 2003). *Accreditation ensures private or public sector organizations that an employee assistance program (EAP) has acceptable level of experience, advisement, and expertise.* Accreditation of Employee Assistance Programs *gives you the information you need to get an employee assistance program accredited. Thorough and focused chapters by respected authorities discuss the value of EAP accreditation to future customers, the development of accreditation standards for employee assistance programs, and the smoothest road to travel to your destination of EAP accreditation.*

Global Perspectives of Occupational Social Work,* edited by R. Paul Maiden, PhD (Vol. 17, No. 1/2, 2001). *A broad survey of the development and current practices of occupational social work as practiced in seven countries around the world.*

Emerging Trends for EAPs in the 21st Century,* edited by Nan Van Den Bergh, PhD, LCSW (Vol. 16, No. 1/2, 2000). *"An excellent book. . . . Relevant with respect to contemporary practice and current state of the art for EAPs. A sound disciplinary input for both program development and service delivery." (William L. Mermis, PhD, Professor of Human Health, Arizona State University)*

Employee Assistance Services in the New South Africa,* edited by R. Paul Maiden, PhD (Vol. 14, No. 3, 1999). *Addresses the many issues affecting the development of EAP programs in the new South Africa.*

Women in the Workplace and Employee Assistance Programs: Perspectives, Innovations, and Techniques for Helping Professionals,* edited by Marta Lundy, PhD, LCSW, and Beverly Younger, MSW, ACSW (Vol. 9, No. 3/4, 1994). *"A valuable resource and training guide to EAP practitioners and managers alike. Most importantly, it increases the sensitivity of women's issues as they relate to the workplace." (R. Paul Maiden, PhD, Chair, Occupational Social Work, Jane Addams College of Social Work, University of Illinois at Chicago)*

Employee Assistance Programs in South Africa,* edited by R. Paul Maiden, MSW (Vol. 7, No. 3, 1992). *"The first comprehensive collection of perspectives on EAPs in an industrializing third-world country." (Brian McKendrick, PhD, Professor and Head, School of Social Work, University of the Witwaterstrand, Johannesburg)*

Occupational Social Work Today,* edited by Shulamith Lala Ashenberg Straussner, DSW, CEAP (Vol. 5, No. 1, 1990). *"A well-organized overview of social work practice in business . . . interesting and timely." (Journal of Clinical Psychiatry)*

Evaluation of Employee Assistance Programs,* edited by Marvin D. Feit, PhD, and Michael J. Holosko, PhD (Vol. 3, No. 3/4, 1989). *"The definitive work in the field of program evaluations of EAPs. . . . A must for anyone considering planning, implementing, and most importantly, evaluating employee assistance programs." (Dr. Gerald Erickson, Professor and Director, School of Social Work, University of Windsor)*

Alcohol in Employment Settings: The Results of the WHO/ILO International Review,* edited by D. Wayne Corneil, ScD (cand.) (Vol. 3, No. 2, 1988). *Valuable insights into attitudes about alcohol and the effects of its use with courses of action for educating and treating employees who need help with alcohol problems.*

EAPs and the Information Revolution: The Dark Side of Megatrends,* edited by Keith McClellan and Richard E. Miller, PhD (Vol. 2, No. 2, 1987). *A serious examination of treatment methods that can be used to help working people cope with a rapidly changing economic society.*

Employee Assistance Programs in Higher Education

R. Paul Maiden, PhD
Sally B. Philips, EdD
Editors

Employee Assistance Programs in Higher Education has been co-published simultaneously as *Journal of Workplace Behavioral Health*, Volume 22, Numbers 2/3, 2006/2007.

The Haworth Press, Inc.

Employee Assistance Programs in Higher Education has been co-published simultaneously as *Journal of Workplace Behavioral Health*, Volume 22, Numbers 2/3, 2006/2007.

Library of Congress Cataloging-in-Publication Data

Employee assistance programs in higher education / R. Paul Maiden, Sally B. Philips, editors.
p. cm.
"Co-published simultaneously as Journal of workplace behavioral health, volume 22, numbers 2/3, 2006/2007."
Includes bibliographical references and index.
ISBN-13: 978-0-7890-3698-8 (hard cover : alk. paper)
ISBN-13: 978-0-7890-3699-5 (soft cover : alk. paper)
1. College personnel management–United States. 2. Employee assistance programs–United States. I. Maiden, R. Paul. II. Philips, Sally B. III. Journal of workplace behavioral health.
LB2331.67.H4E478 2008
378.1′1–dc22

2008000048

The HAWORTH PRESS

Abstracting, Indexing & Outward Linking

PRINT *and* ELECTRONIC BOOKS & JOURNALS

This section provides you with a list of major indexing & abstracting services and other tools for bibliographic access. That is to say, each service began covering this periodical during the year noted in the right column. Most Websites which are listed below have indicated that they will either post, disseminate, compile, archive, cite or alert their own Website users with research-based content from this work. (This list is as current as the copyright date of this publication.)

Abstracting, Website/Indexing Coverage . . . . Year When Coverage Began

- ***Academic Search Premier (EBSCO) <http://search.ebscohost.com>*** **2006**
- ***Academic Source Premier (EBSCO) <http://search.ebscohost.com>*** **2007**
- ***Addiction Abstracts (Published in collaboration with the National Addiction Centre & Carfax, Taylor & Francis) <http://www.tandf.co.uk/addiction-abs>*** **2007**
- ***Advanced Polymers Abstracts (ProQuest CSA) <http://www.csa.com/factsheets/ema-polymers-set-c.php>*** **2007**
- ***Alcohol Studies Database <http://cf7-test.scc-net.rutgers.edu/alcohol_studies/alcohol/index.htm>*** **2007**
- ***BEFO <http://www.fiz-technik.de/en_db/d_befo.htm>*** **2006**
- ***British Library Inside (The British Library) <http://www.bl.uk/services/current/inside.html>*** **2006**
- ***Business Source Complete (EBSCO) <http://search.ebscohost.com>*** **2006**
- ***Business Source Premier (EBSCO) <http://search.ebscohost.com>*** **2006**
- ***Cambridge Scientific Abstracts (ProQuest CSA) <http://www.csa.com>*** **2006**
- ***Ceramic Abstracts (ProQuest CSA) <http://www.csa.com/factsheets/wca-set-c.php>*** **2007**
- ***Composites Industry Abstracts (ProQuest CSA) <http://www.csa.com/factsheets/ema-composites-set-c.php>*** . . . **2007**

(continued)

- *Computer and Information Systems Abstracts (ProQuest CSA)*
  <http://www.csa.com/factsheets/computer-set-c.php> **2007**
- *Corrosion Abstracts (ProQuest CSA)*
  <http://www.csa.com/factsheets/corrosion-set-c.php> **2007**
- *CSA Engineering Research Database (ProQuest CSA)*
  <http://www.csa.com/factsheets/engineering-set-c.php> **2007**
- *CSA High Technology Research Database With Aerospace (ProQuest CSA)*
  <http://www.csa.com/factsheets/hightech-set-c.php> **2007**
- *CSA Technology Research Database (ProQuest CSA)*
  <http://www.csa.com/factsheets/techresearch-set-c.php>. **2007**
- *CSA/ASCE Civil Engineering Abstracts (ProQuest CSA)*
  <http://www.csa.com/factsheets/civil-set-c.php>. **2007**
- *Current Abstracts (EBSCO) <http://search.ebscohost.com>* **2007**
- *EAP Abstracts Plus <http://www.eaptechnology.com>* **1994**
- *EBSCOhost Electronic Journals Service (EJS)*
  <http://search.ebscohost.com>. **2001**
- *Education Research Complete (EBSCO)*
  <http://search.ebscohost.com>. **2006**
- *Education Research Index (EBSCO)*
  <http://search.ebscohost.com>. **2007**
- *Electronic Collections Online (OCLC)*
  <http://www.oclc.org/electroniccollections/> **2006**
- *Electronics and Communications Abstracts (ProQuest CSA)*
  <http://www.csa.com/factsheets/electronics-set-c.php> **2007**
- *Elsevier Eflow -D <http://www.elsevier.com>* **2006**
- *Elsevier Scopus <http://www.info.scopus.com>* **2005**
- *Engineered Materials Abstracts (ProQuest CSA)*
  <http://www.csa.com/factsheets/emaclust-set-c.php>. **2007**
- *Entrepreneurship Research Engine*
  <http://research.kauffman.org> **2004**
- *Family & Society Studies Worldwide (NISC USA)*
  <http://www.nisc.com>. **1996**
- *Family Index Database <http://www.familyscholar.com>* **2004**
- *Family Violence & Sexual Assault Bulletin>* **2006**
- *Google <http://www.google.com>*. **2004**
- *Google Scholar <http://scholar.google.com>* **2004**
- *Haworth Document Delivery Center*
  <http://www.HaworthPress.com/journals/dds.asp> **2004**

(continued)

- *Health & Psychosocial Instruments (HaPI) Database>* **1999**
- *Human Resources Abstracts (Sage)* **1985**
- *ILO/BIT-CIS Bulletin* **2006**
- *Index to Periodical Articles Related to Law <http://www.law.utexas.edu>* **1985**
- *IndexCopernicus <http://www.indexcopernicus.com>* **2007**
- *Information for Practice <http://www.nyu.edu/socialwork/ip/>* . . . **2007**
- *International Abstracts of Human Resources <http://www.humanresourcesabstracts.com/journals.php>* **1988**
- *International Bibliography of Periodical Literature on the Humanities and Social Sciences (IBZ) (Thomson) <http://www.saur.de>* **2001**
- *Internationale Bibliographie der geistes- und sozialwissenschaftlichen Zeitschriftenliteratur (See IBZ) <http://www.saur.de>* **2001**
- *JournalSeek <http://www.journalseek.net>* **2006**
- *Links@Ovid (via CrossRef targeted DOI links) <http://www.ovid.com>* **2005**
- *MasterFILE Premier (EBSCO) <http://search.ebscohost.com>* . . . **2006**
- *Materials Business File (ProQuest CSA) <http://www.csa.com/factsheets/mbf-set-c.php>* **2007**
- *Materials Research Database with METADEX (ProQuest CSA) <http://www.csa.com/factsheets/materials-set-c.php>* **2007**
- *Mechanical & Transportation Engineering Abstracts (ProQuest CSA) <http://www.csa.com/factsheets/mechtrans-set-c.php>* **2007**
- *Medical Benefits <http://www.aspenpublishers.com>* **2002**
- *METADEX (ProQuest CSA) <http://www.csa.com/factsheets/metadex-set-c.php>* **2007**
- *NewJour (Electronic Journals & Newsletters) <http://gort.ucsd.edu/newjour/>* **2006**
- *OCLC ArticleFirst <http://www.oclc.org/services/databases/>* **2007**
- *Ovid Linksolver (OpenURL link resolver via CrossRef targeted DOI links) <http://www.linksolver.com>* **2005**
- *Professional Development Collection (EBSCO) <http://search.ebscohost.com>* **2006**
- *Psychological Abstracts (PsycINFO) <http://www.apa.org>* **1985**
- *Referativnyi Zhurnal (Abstracts Journal of the All-Russian Institute of Scientific and Technical Information–in Russian) <http://www.viniti.ru>* **2006**
- *SALIS (Substance Abuse Librarians & Information Specialists) Alcohol, Tobacco & Other Drug Journals on the Web <http://www.salis.org/resources/atod_journals.html>* **2007**

(continued)

- *Scopus (See instead Elsevier Scopus)* *<http://www.info.scopus.com>* **2005**
- *Social Services Abstracts (ProQuest CSA)* *<http://www.csa.com>* **2006**
- *Social Work Abstracts (NASW)* *<http://www.silverplatter.com/catalog/swab.htm>* **1988**
- *SocINDEX with Full Text (EBSCO)* *<http://search.ebscohost.com>* **2007**
- *Sociological Abstracts (ProQuest CSA)* *<http://www.csa.com>* **2007**
- *Solid State and Superconductivity Abstracts (ProQuest CSA)* *<http://www.csa.com/factsheets/solid-state-set-c.php>* **2007**
- *TOC Premier (EBSCO) <http://search.ebscohost.com>* **2007**
- *zetoc (The British Library) <http://www.bl.uk>* **2004**

Bibliographic Access

- ***Cabell's Directory of Publishing Opportunities in Management <http://www.cabells.com>***
- ***MediaFinder <http://www.mediafinder.com/>***
- ***Ulrich's Periodicals Directory: The Global Source for Periodicals Information Since 1932 <http://www.bowkerlink.com>***

Special Bibliographic Notes related to special journal issues (separates) and indexing/abstracting:

- indexing/abstracting services in this list will also cover material in any "separate" that is co-published simultaneously with Haworth's special thematic journal issue or DocuSerial. Indexing/abstracting usually covers material at the article/chapter level.
- monographic co-editions are intended for either non-subscribers or libraries which intend to purchase a second copy for their circulating collections.
- monographic co-editions are reported to all jobbers/wholesalers/approval plans. The source journal is listed as the "series" to assist the prevention of duplicate purchasing in the same manner utilized for books-in-series.
- to facilitate user/access services all indexing/abstracting services are encouraged to utilize the co-indexing entry note indicated at the bottom of the first page of each article/chapter/contribution.
- this is intended to assist a library user of any reference tool (whether print, electronic, online, or CD-ROM) to locate the monographic version if the library has purchased this version but not a subscription to the source journal.
- individual articles/chapters in any Haworth publication are also available through the Haworth Document Delivery Service (HDDS).

∞ ALL HAWORTH BOOKS AND JOURNALS
ARE PRINTED ON CERTIFIED
ACID-FREE PAPER

Employee Assistance Programs in Higher Education

CONTENTS

ABOUT THE EDITORS

R. Paul Maiden, PhD, is the editor of the *Journal of Workplace Behavioral Health.* He is also Associate Professor of social work at the University of Central Florida in Orlando. He is a recipient of two Senior Fulbright Scholar awards to Russia and South Africa. He has been in the EAP field for 25 years and has an extensive portfolio of domestic and international publications, presentations and consultations on a wide range of workplace human service issues. He is editor and contributing author of *Employee Assistance Programs in South Africa, Total Quality Management in EAPs, Global Perspectives of Occupational Social Work, Employee Assistance Services in the New South Africa, Accreditation of Employee Assistance Programs*, and *The Integration of Employee Assistance, Work/Life, and Wellness Services* (with Attridge and Herlihy).

Sally B. Philips, EdD, has been working in the EAP field for more than 20 years. She is currently, the director of the Employee Assistance Program (EAP) at the University of Miami. Prior to joining the University of Miami, Dr. Philips was employed with an EAP provider in the Wall Street area of New York City.

Dr. Philips is active in several EAP professional associations. From 2003 to 2004 she was president of IAEAPE (International Association of Employee Assistance Professionals in Education) and was the IAEAPE Treasurer from 2005-2006. She also coordinates educational programs of the South Florida EAPA (Employee Assistance Professionals Association) chapter. While in New York City, she was on the program committee of that EAPA chapter. Dr. Philips earned an AB at Cornell University and an EdM in Counselor Education and EdD in Counseling Psychology at Boston University. Dr. Philips has published for the American Psychological Association, the Journal of Workplace Behavioral Health, the Employee Assistance Quarterly and the VRA Bulletin. She has also presented at numerous employee assistance and other human resource related conferences throughout her EAP career.

About the Contributors

Deborah Adiego Cagnon, MSW, is a Licensed Clinical Social Worker and a Certified Employee Assistance Professional. She has worked in the Employee Assistance field for over ten years working for both internal and external programs including corporate and academic settings. She currently works for Kaiser Permanente Medical Center in Vallejo, California (E-mail: deborah.adiego-cagnon@kp.org).

Donna L. Buehler, MS, is Director of Stony Brook University Employee Assistance Program. She has expertise in both internal and external EAPs in academic, healthcare, union and corporate organizations since 1985. She was Program Coordinator of the Vanderbilt Institute for Treatment of Addiction Outpatient Program for seven years. Ms. Buehler has taught several graduate social work courses at The University of Tennessee School of Social Work–Nashville branch and lectured at Vanderbilt School of Nursing and Stony Brook University School of Social Welfare Geriatric Care Manager Program. She is a graduate of Columbia University School of Social Work (E-mail: dbuehler@notes.cc.sunysb.edu).

Rick Csiernik, PhD, is Professor and Graduate Program Coordinator at the School of Social Work, King's University College at The University of Western Ontario, London, Ontario where he teaches Research, Group Work, Field Practice and Addictions. Rick is the author of over 70 peer reviewed articles and book chapters and has written and edited three books including *Wellness and Work: Employee Assistance Programming in Canada* as well as being an invited and peer reviewed presenter to over 100 national and international conferences, seminars and workshops. Rick was co-developer of the EAP Studies Diploma Program at McMaster University, Hamilton, Ontario the first of its kind in Canada and continues to teach in the Addiction Studies program where he was recipient of the Instructor of the Year Award in 1997. He has also been on the Dean's Honour Roll of Teaching Excellence at King's University College on eight separate occasions (E-mail: rcsierni@uwo.ca).

John B. Franz, PhD, is currently Professor and BA Program Coordinator in the Department of Social Work Education at California State University,

Fresno. He formerly served as the Director of his campus' Employee Assistance & Development office (E-mail: johnfr@csufresno.edu).

Margie Gale, MSN, joined the staff in September 2002 as the Nurse Wellness Specialist to coordinate the Nurse Wellness Program efforts. Margie has been an RN since 1973. She is also a Mental Health Clinical Nurse Specialist having been in private clinical practice, a nursing instructor at the Vanderbilt School of Nursing, Meharry Medical College and at Columbia State Community College, and a consultant for several community programs (E-mail: Margie.gale@vanderbily.edu).

Bruce Goya, MEd, is a Program Coordinator at the University of California, Office of the President. He provides system wide coordination for Rehabilitation Programs and Employee Assistance Programs, and serves as program administrator for behavioral health care benefits. He has presented at national conferences for the Washington Business Group on Health, the Employee Assistance Professionals Association, and the Alliance of Work-Life Progress (E-mail: bruce.goya@ucop.edu).

David Hannah, PhD, has wide-ranging experience in a variety of areas of student and registrarial services in Alberta, British Columbia, and Saskatchewan. He has worked as an advisor, counsellor, registrar, and college/university administrator, has led the implementation of student information systems at three institutions, and participated in the start-up of a college in the Middle East and of the Technical University of British Colombia. In 2002 he was appointed Associate Vice-President, Student and Enrolment Services at the University of Saskatchewan. He is the author of "Postsecondary Students and the Courts in Canada: Cases and Commentary from the Common Law Provinces" (1998) (E-mail: David.hannah@usask.ca).

Susan Harnden, MSW, has been a clinical social worker at the UT EAP for thirteen years. She specializes in communication and relationship problems. She has conducted workshops on various topics including, substance abuse, parenting, self-esteem, and communication for numerous community and educational organizations. Susan serves as a communication consultant for divisions and departments across the UT campus and has a private counseling practice in Austin. Contact information: University of Texas at Austin, Employee Assistance Program, P.O. Box 8060 Austin, TX 78713 (E-mail: susan.harnden@austin.utexas.edu).

Carol Hoffman, MSW, is the Manager, Work/Life at UC Berkeley. Prior to this, she founded and directed two employee assistance programs, at Kaiser Permanente Medical Center, San Francisco, and UC Berkeley (for faculty and staff). Carol currently participates on the Employee Assistance

Professionals Association (EAPA) Work/Life Committee, College and University Work/Family Association (CUWFA) Board of Directors, and the Advisory Council of One Small Step, the SF-Bay Area Employer Work/Life Organization. She has presented at many conferences and has been published in a number of publications on various work/life and EAP topics including elder care, trauma, disaster, and deaths (E-mail: choffman@uhs.berkeley.edu).

Daniel Hughes, PhD, is a New York State Licensed Clinical Social Worker (LCSW-R) and a Certified Employee Assistance Professional (CEAP). Presently, he is the Director of the Mt. Sinai Medical Center's Employee Assistance Program (EAP) and an Assistant Professor of Community and Preventive Medicine, Mt. Sinai School of Medicine. Dr. Hughes has been a member of Boston College's Work Family Roundtable representing the Mt. Sinai-NYU Health System. He is the immediate-past President of the NYC Chapter of the Employee Assistance Professional Association (EAPA) and the current chair of EAPA's research sub-committee. Lastly, Dr. Hughes serves as a member of the Mt. Sinai Medical Center's Physician Wellness Committee (PWC). Accordingly, he participates in investigations and interventions involving impaired medical practice (E-mail: Daniel.Hughes@mssm.edu).

Jim Kendall, MSW, joined Work/Life Connections-EAP at Vanderbilt University in Nashville in 2000 as Manager. He is a Licensed Clinical Social Worker who earned his MSSW at the University Of Tennessee College of Social Work in 1978 after completing his undergraduate studies at the University of California at Santa Cruz. Jim was the 2005 "Friend of Nursing" Award winner (E-mail: james.kendall@bvanderbilt.edu).

Teresa Kulper, MSW, is the Director of Faculty and Staff Services and a workplace organizational consultant at the University of Iowa (UI). Faculty and Staff Services administers the UI Employee Assistance Program (EAP), the Behavior Risk Management Program and the Organizational Effectiveness Consultation program. She recently completed certificate programs in Advanced Organizational Development and Bottom Line Organizational Development: A Structured Process for Increasing Return on Investment. Teresa has 21 years of experience working with internal and external EAP programs. This has afforded her the opportunity to work with employees, supervisors and administrators on issues such as organizational development, process improvement, healthy workforce, team building, workplace violence, training supervisors to build positive work environments, leadership development, and developing and maintaining positive work relationships (E-mail: teresa-kupler@uiowa.edu).

James Pender, PhD, is currently a principal with *Byrnes, Pender & Associates*, a provider of integrated Occupational Health and Employee & Family Assistance Program services. He has completed four degrees including a Master of Social Work (Clinical Specialization) and a PhD in Educational Research. Jim has worked in the transportation, agricultural, educational, oil & gas, and professional services sectors and has held senior human resources positions in the areas of Organizational Development, Performance Management, and Employee Assistance. He is a current member of the board of directors for the Calgary Women's Emergency Shelter and is a member of the Association of Collaborative Professionals (Calgary). In addition to this, he is a past member of the Board of Directors for the Alberta Law Foundation, the Alberta Adolescent Recovery Centre (AARC), and the Family Resource Centre (E-mail: jpender@byrnespender.com).

Sally B. Philips, EdD, has worked in employee assistance programs since 1984. She has held various positions in three EAPs. Dr. Philips earned an AB at Cornell University where she majored in English. She received an EdM in Counselor Education and doctorate in Counseling Psychology from Boston University. Dr. Philips is licensed as a psychologist in Massachusetts, New York and Florida. She became a Certified Employee Assistance Professional in 1988. Since April 1997, she has been directing the Employee Assistance Program at the University of Miami. She has held officer positions in the International Association of Employee Assistance Professionals in Education (IAEAPE) and been active in local chapters of EAPA (E-mail: sally@miami.edu).

Amanda L. Price, PhD, is a Clinicial Associate Faculty member of Occupational Medicine at Duke University Medical Center and is a counselor for Duke Personal Assistance Service at Duke University and Health System (E-mail: price065@mc.duke.edu).

Mary E. Remón, LMHC, CEAP, staffs the EAP office at University of Miami's Miller School of Medicine. An active member of IAEAPE, Mary currently serves as the board secretary and membership committee liaison. She was co-chair of the IAEAPE 2005 conference program committee, and presented at the 2004 and 2006 annual conferences. Mary is also actively involved in the EAPA/South Florida chapter. She is bilingual in English and Spanish, and has prior experience working in crisis center, managed care and university settings (E-mail: mremon@miami.edu).

Theodore A. Rice, MEd, joined as a clinical counselor for the Work/Life Connections-EAP in 2004. Ted received a BA in Psychology from Marshall University in Huntington, West Virginia in 1994 and a Master's in Education degree in Human Developmental Counseling at Vanderbilt University in 1997. Ted Rice is a National Board Certified Counselor, as well as a Licensed Professional Counselor, Mental Health Service Provider Status designation, in the state of Tennessee (E-mail: Theodore.a.rice@ vanderbilt.edu).

Monica Scamardo, PsyD, is a licensed psychologist at the UT EAP where she works with professional and personal challenges related to managing change, reactions and stress; relationship/interpersonal problems; and goal-setting and achievement. She consults with and coaches managers and employees dealing with workplace problems, change management, and leadership development. Monica is also the president of Variate Consulting, a coaching and training firm that specializes in organizational and human resource development (E-mail: monica.scamardo@austin.utexas.edu).

Joel Shapiro, MSW, is the Director of the University of Vermont Employee Assistance and Lifetime Wellness Programs (E-mail: Joel.Shapiro@ uvm.edu).

Andrew S. Silberman, MSW, is an Assistant Clinical Professor of Occupational Medicine at Duke University Medical Center and Director of Personal Assistance Service at Duke University and Health System (E-Mail: andrew.silberman@duke.edu).

David L. Swihart, MA, is the Employee Assistance Coordinator for the University of Arizona, serving in the integrated UA Life & Work Connections program. Besides providing employee assistance services, Dave is also a frequent presenter to university groups, and at the state and national levels on a variety of topics related to emotional health, wellness, and life cycle balance. Dave's background includes work as a clinician in community and other non-profit mental health agencies (E-mail: dswihart@ email.arizona.edu).

Darci A. Thompson, MSW, is the director of UA Life & Work Connections, an integrated employee assistance, wellness, and work/life program at the University of Arizona. Darci has 20 years in higher education, focusing on strategic organizational growth and leveraging interdisciplinary teams. Additionally, she is a business consultant regarding employee life cycle services, a program developer, emphasizing the health resiliency approach to client services, and an educator and field liaison for undergraduate and graduate students in social work. Darci has been a presenter to national, state, and local conferences, and holds a bachelor's degree in communications and marketing from the University of Arizona and a master's degree in social work from Arizona State University (E-mail: darci@ email.arizona.edu).

Ellen Trice, MBA, MSW, was recruited to be the first full time EAP at Vanderbilt in 1992. She serves as the Clinical Manager. Ellen earned her BS from Peabody in Human Behavior and her MBA from Vanderbilt University. She completed her Master's degree in Social Work from the University of Tennessee. She is a licensed clinical social worker and certified as an EAP professional and social worker (E-mail: ellen.trice@vanderbilt.edu).

Thomas R. Waldecker, MSW, is the Director of the Faculty and Staff Assistance Program for the University of Michigan and has held that position since 1998. Prior to that he was a Regional Manager for Managed Health Network, where he directed the EAP to over 33,000 Ford Motor Company salaried employees. Additionally, while at MHN he was responsible for managing the EAPs for several other large corporate accounts, including the Stroh Brewery Company, Lincoln National Insurance, and others. Prior to that, he was an EAP counselor in several settings, including the Kelsey Hayes Company. He has over twenty six years of EAP experience. Mr. Waldecker received his MSW from the University of Michigan. Currently Tom is the Chair of the International Association of Employee Assistance Professionals in Education (IAEAPE) Membership Committee and previously served on their executive board. He is also a member of the American College of Mental Health Administration (E-mail: tomwal@umich.edu).

Mary Yarbrough, MD, MPH, is the Director of Health and Wellness Programs including the Work/Life Connections-EAP, including Faculty, Physician and Nurse Wellness Programs,Occupational Health Clinic; the Child and Family Center, and HEALTH *Plus*, Vanderbilt's health promotion program. She received her BSc in Biomedical Engineering and her MD from Vanderbilt University. Dr. Yarbrough completed her residency in Internal Medicine at Vanderbilt and in Preventive Medicine at Johns Hopkins University. She is an Assistant Professor of both Medicine and Preventive Medicine at Vanderbilt (E-mail: mary.yarborough@vanderbilt.edu).

Preface: The Industry and Community of Academe

Academia is a unique industry and universities are a form of a diverse community. Take a stroll across any college or university campus in the world and enter any building and one will encounter a continual flurry of activity–sometimes loud and boisterous, other times sedate and studious. Academia is also an extremely diversified community of individuals–administrators and support staff, faculty instructors and researchers, buildings and grounds maintenance workers, and students from all points of the globe representing most ethnic groups and speaking a myriad of languages.

With 25 years spent as a university professor I have found that academia is a place of great stimulation and excitement when one is engaged in teaching, research and service but is also sometimes, in equal measure, a place of stress, anxiety and upheaval for individuals who are often driven to achieve and build reputations of excellence and recognition among their peers.

Academia can be quite deceptive. To the individual *on the outside looking in* employment in a university environment is a workplace ideal and, in many ways it is. A university grants faculty members considerable autonomy in their work life while on the other hand demands continual excellence in teaching, research and scholarship production. While the university culture is quite different from most other work settings the needs of this diverse workplace are essentially the same.

EAPs in Academe focuses on the unique aspects and challenges of employee assistance service delivery in a university environment. Joel Shapiro and Sally Philips begin with an overview of the development of EAPs in academic settings and also provide a review of the International Association of Employee Assistance Programs in Education (IAEAPE), the professional association for university based EAP practitioners.

[Haworth co-indexing entry note]: "Preface: The Industry and Community of Academe." Maiden, R. Paul. Co-published simultaneously in *Journal of Workplace Behavioral Health* (The Haworth Press, Inc.) Vol. 22, No. 2/3, 2006/2007, pp. xxxi-xxxiii; and: *Employee Assistance Programs in Higher Education* (ed: R. Paul Maiden, and Sally B. Philips) The Haworth Press, Inc., 2006/2007, pp. xxiii-xxv. Single or multiple copies of this article are available for a fee from The Haworth Document Delivery Service [1-800-HAWORTH, 9:00 a.m. - 5:00 p.m. (EST). E-mail address: docdelivery@haworthpress.com].

Available online at http://jwbh.haworthpress.com

Sally Philips, Deborah Adiego Cagnon, Donna L. Buehler, Mary Remón and Thomas R. Waldecker in their article *Academic and Corporate Cultures Contrasted* . . . identify and discuss key cultural and organizational differences between academic institutions and corporate employers and how these differences influence the administration of a university based employee assistance program.

Daniel Hughes, in his article on *University Based Employee Assistance Programs and Outsourcing* . . . , explores the emerging trend of outsourcing as way of reducing costs. Hughes argues that established university based EAPs often reflect the unique culture of the academic workplace, an aspect that will likely be lost (to the detriment of the university) if EAP services are outsourced to providers who are not part or cognizant of the culture of academia.

Rick Csiernik, David Hannah and James Pender in their article, *Change, Evolution and Adaptation of a University EAP* . . . explore the decision making of administrators and consultants at the University of Saskatchewan who engaged in a planning and development exercise as a means of assessing the value of the EAP to their university community in comparison to 12 other Canadian universities. The end result was the creation of a substantial strategic change plan for this university's employee assistance program.

John B. Franz's article on *Enhancing Faculty Access: A Cultural Challenge for EAPs in Academe* addresses some of the unique aspects of working with a faculty work force that is highly autonomous and generally receives little direct supervision from their department chairs. Franz also examines factors that explain faculty resistance to accessing EAPs and identifies strategies that university based programs can use to overcome some of this resistance.

Teresa Kulper's article titled *Beyond Management Consultation: Partnering with Human Resources for Organizational Effectiveness* explores the need for and development of enhanced management consultation in employee assistance programs in university settings. Kulper discusses her experiences in developing partnerships between the EAP and human resources at the University of Iowa using a systems perspective in dealing with organizational and interpersonal problems.

Andrew Silberman, James W. Kendall, Amanda L. Price and Theodore A. Rice, EAP practitioners at Duke and Vanderbilt, in their article on *University Employee Assistance Programs Response to Trauma on Campus* demonstrate that the academic workplace is no exception when it comes to trauma and violence but do point out that responding to the diverse constituency of university employees does create a unique set of challenges.

James Kendall, Theodore A. Rice, Margie Gale, Ellen Trice, and Mary I. Yarbrough in their article on *The Creation of a Specialized University EAP Program–A Nurse Wellness Program* describes the development of a program focusing on the unique needs of nurses in Vanderbilt university's medical center. The authors identify the unique set of stressors faced by nurses and discuss the development of a specialized nurse wellness program to help manage these stressors.

Monica Scamardo and Susan C. Harnden in their article, *A Manager Coaching Group Model . . .* discuss the challenges and benefits of a coaching and support group for managers that they developed through their EAP at the University of Texas at Austin. They suggest that EAP facilitation of manager groups can help reduce managers' stress and build their supportive and professional networks while helping to develop managers' communication and "soft skills."

The last two articles appearing in this volume are reprints and were first published in *The Integration of Employee Assistance, Work/Life and Wellness* (Attridge, Herlihy and Maiden, 2005). Given the thematic focus of this volume on *EAPs in Academe* I thought it apropos that these two works from EAP professionals at the University of Arizona and the University of California–Berkley be include in this volume.

Darci Thompson and David Swihart who staff the University of Arizona Work and Life Connections program discuss how this academic program was conceptualized and implemented from its' inception as a fully integrated model rather than going through the traditional evolution of employee assistance to work/life.

Carol Hoffman and Bruce Goya describe a specifically designed initiative to address the deaths of faculty, staff, and students at the University of California at Berkeley. Their model framework is presented to demonstrate the vital need for coordination and integration among many of the employers' programs, services, and activities in order to address workplace deaths.

After reading this series of articles from employee assistance professionals plying their trade in some of the leading American universities, one will no doubt more fully appreciate the workplace aspects specific to academia. One is also bound to become more cognizant of some of the challenges of managing an EAP in educational settings that are, in essence, unique free standing communities.

R. Paul Maiden, PhD
University of Central Florida
School of Social Work

History and Evolution of the International Association of Employee Assistance Professionals in Education (IAEAPE)

Joel Shapiro
Sally B. Philips

SUMMARY. This article provides an historical overview of the evolution of the International Association of Employee Assistance Professionals in Education (IAEAPE). The IAEAPE was developed in parallel with the introduction of employee assistance programs in higher education. doi:10.1300/J490v22n03_01 *[Article copies available for a fee from The Haworth Document Delivery Service: 1-800-HAWORTH. E-mail address: <docdelivery@haworthpress.com> Website: <http://www.HaworthPress.com> © 2006/2007 by The Haworth Press, Inc. All rights reserved.]*

KEYWORDS. IAEAPE, EAP, International Association of Employee Assistance Professionals in Education

---

[Haworth co-indexing entry note]: "History and Evolution of the International Association of Employee Assistance Professionals in Education (IAEAPE)." Shapiro, Joel and Sally B. Philips. Co-published simultaneously in *Journal of Workplace Behavioral Health* (The Haworth Press, Inc.) Vol. 22, No. 2/3, 2006/2007, pp. 1-5; and: *Employee Assistance Programs in Higher Education* (ed: R. Paul Maiden and Sally B. Philips) The Haworth Press, 2006/2007, pp. 1-5. Single or multiple copies of this article are available for a fee from The Haworth Document Delivery Service [1-800-HAWORTH, 9:00 a.m. - 5:00 p.m. (EST). E-mail address: docdelivery@haworthpress.com].

Available online at http://jwbh.haworthpress.com

doi:10.1300/J490v22n03_01

INTRODUCTION

Roots in Industrial Alcohol Programs

Employee Assistance programming expanded from industry to higher education with the development of three higher education employee assistance programs (EAPs) in the mid 1970s. During this time, the University of Delaware, Rutgers University, and the University of Missouri initiated programs to handle alcohol abuse by faculty and staff. In 1976, with the support of a National Institute of Alcohol Abuse and Alcoholism (NIAA) grant, the University of Missouri sponsored the first of six conferences designed to assist institutions of higher education in establishing EAPs.

After the NIAA support ended in 1982, a number of individuals in EAPs in educational settings, including K-12, community colleges and universities, agreed to continue meeting to share ideas. Initially called "EAPs in Education" the group met from 1982 through 1992. They formally organized as an association in 1993: "The International Association of Employee Assistance Professionals in Education" (IAEAPE). The IAEAPE operates independently of other EAP associations. Currently the organization has over 150 members from 80 institutions.

PHASES OF DEVELOPMENT

Phase One

In an article titled "The College and University EAP Network" (1990), IAEAPE member Dr. William Mermis described the several distinct phases of the development of EAPs in education which led to the formation of the IAEAPE.

The first phase occurred in the mid 1970s. While business and industry were involved for many years with employee assistance programs (which often were primarily alcohol assistance programs), the same was not true for EAPs in educational settings. A crucial turning point in this development started in the mid 1970s.

A major force (leading to the development of EAPs in higher education) was the NIAAA grants made to the University of Missouri at Columbia during the years 1976 to 1981 . . . at the time of their first grant, there were probably less than 10 programs in higher education settings. (Mermis, 1990)

Annual Conferences

These first grants from NIAAA were part of a funding strategy to develop a network of colleges and universities EAPs. As a result of these grants, Drs. Richard Thorenson and Elizabeth Hosokawa of the University of Missouri at Columbia spearheaded a series of conferences beginning in August 1976 and continuing through 1981. The first conference occurred in Columbia, Missouri. Then, the conference site moved to other cities. These conference proceedings were the forerunner of the annual IAEAPE conferences that continues today. By 1990 approximately 200 programs existed in universities and colleges as a result of this initial seeding.

From the oral history we know these meetings established the tone of mutual support, information sharing and creative brainstorming which remain core values of IAEAPE. These individuals, responsible for operating EAPs in an academic setting recognized that operating within an academic culture created some unique practical and ethical issues. It has been well documented that the culture and structure of higher education especially within the faculty, is having the flexibility of time and schedule to explore, conduct research, create innovative programs, investigate new ideas and develop new protocols. . . The freedom to be creative that is essential to these activities can also provide protection for those who need assistance and are non productive members. . .Because deteriorating job performance is more difficult to monitor and detect in terms of faculty performance especially at the level of tenured professor or dean, it can be less useful as a criterion on which to base a referral to an EAP. (Stoers-Scagg, 1999).

Additionally, the academic culture includes academically trained individuals performing managerial roles in a shared decision making context. Most campus communities are essentially mini-cities with the infrastructure needed to maintain housing, security, food and educational resources for its students, meaning a 24-hour staffed system. Many universities are affiliated with medical colleges and teaching hospitals, adding another population base with important needs to be served. Consequently, these programs serve a wide diversity of people and reflect several organizational sub cultures. Having a venue to discuss how to institute and successfully operate an EAP in a university or college setting became a vital component of the annual conferences.

Phase Two

The second phase of the development of EAPs in Higher Education, which eventually led to the formal establishment of IAEAPE, was a series of conferences coordinated with the annual Employee Assistance Professionals Association (EAPA) conference. Informally calling themselves "EAPs in Education," the group met annually from 1982 to 1991. It became a tradition that the university from the host city took a key role in organizing the conference. The conference and gatherings would meet for the day or two preceding the national EAPA conference. These conferences continued the tradition of fostering discussion on issues pertinent to higher education and became a rich resource for networking and sharing information.

Other Concerns

Simultaneously, the development of EAPs in K-12 education became organized and members from this group joined the IAEAPE and assumed some leadership positions. In addition, the association wrestled during this period with formally aligning itself with either EAPA or Employee Assistance Society of North America (EASNA).

Phase Three

The third phase began with the decision to formally organize "EAPs in Education" as IAEAPE (International Association of EAPs in Education). Dr. Polly Moutevelis-Karris from the University of Maine was the organization's President during this transition period.

Communication Modes

IAEAPE has grown and thrived during the past 12 years. The annual conference has provided a regular opportunity for sharing information and strategies. We developed a website (www.iaeape.org) with a section open to the public. The members-only section contains a wealth of information on presentations, policy development, trainings, responses to list serve polls, etc. A directory that compiled information on all members was published each year, as was a semi-annual newsletter. Since 2004 the IAEAPE directory has been on line at the web site. A list serve, spearheaded by Fran Deats from the University of Massachusetts, was started in 2001. It has provided another rich resource for sharing of information and support. It has allowed us to stay virtually connected to such an extent that the twice a year newsletter was discontinued in 2003.

Virtual Headquarters

Indeed, electronic technology has made it possible for this small association to carry on its business in a virtual setting. IAEAPE has no headquarters. Currently, the four-officer Board meets monthly through a conference call. The membership has access to these minutes via the members-only section of the web site. When input is needed from all the members, the officers communicate through the listserv instead of a convened meeting. The annual business meeting of the membership which is required by the Bylaws is scheduled during the annual conference. Thanks to long-standing cooperation with US Bank, checking account activity is done by mail, and statements are downloaded from the Internet. The TIAA-CREF saving account statements are also retrieved from the Internet. Each officer at the end of his or her term forwards to his or her replacement the essential documents that inform that office.

REFERENCES

Mermis, William. (1990, February). The college and university EAP network, *EAPA Exchange*, 34-35.

Stoer-Scaggs, L. (1999). Employee assistance programs in higher education. In Oher, J. (Ed.), The *employee assistance handbook* (pp. 35-58). New York: Wiley.

doi:10.1300/J490v22n03_01

Academic and Corporate Cultures Contrasted: Implications for Employee Assistance Professionals

Sally B. Philips
Deborah Adiego Cagnon
Donna L. Buehler
Mary E. Remón
Thomas R. Waldecker

SUMMARY. The purpose of this article is to acquaint employee assistance professionals with some of the cultural differences between academic institutions and corporate employers. The authors will describe how these differences affect the provision of employee assistance services. Four key differences are identified. The first is exemplified in the respective mission statements adopted by academic institutions and business corporations. A second difference is that educational institutions are far more accepting of diversity of thought and more likely to respond to or investigate complaints. In contrast, corporate culture often dictates that the hierarchy not be challenged. The third is in the area of decision making. In academic settings decision making is most often done by a committee consensus process. Consequently, it is very slow. In a corporate setting decisions are made by a few key people. As a result, changes suggested by employee assistance practitioners are more likely to be more challenging to implement in academic settings than in corporations. The final difference between the two cultures is that a large segment of the academic work force is minimally supervised. Relative to

[Haworth co-indexing entry note]: "Academic and Corporate Cultures Contrasted: Implications for Employee Assistance Professionals." Philips, Sally B., et al. Co-published simultaneously in *Journal of Workplace Behavioral Health* (The Haworth Press, Inc.) Vol. 22, No. 2/3, 2006/2007, pp. 7-25; and: *Employee Assistance Programs in Higher Education* (ed: R. Paul Maiden and Sally B. Philips) The Haworth Press, 2006/2007, pp. 7-25. Single or multiple copies of this article are available for a fee from The Haworth Document Delivery Service [1-800-HAWORTH, 9:00 a.m. - 5:00 p.m. (EST). E-mail address: docdelivery@haworthpress.com].

Available online at http://jwbh.haworthpress.com

doi:10.1300/J490v22n03_02

corporate America, this segment is not held as accountable for its performance or conduct. Traditionally, employee assistance professionals advise supervisors to use "consequences" as tools to motivate behavior change. However, such advice is nearly meaningless when targeted to this quarter to a third of an academic institution's employee population. Some alternative motivational techniques are outlined. doi:10.1300/J490v22n03_02

KEYWORDS. EAP, academia, academic culture, corporate culture, higher education

INTRODUCTION

Recently Geoffrey Marczyk likened an organization's culture to an individual's personality: "It provides shared meaning, communicates expectations and establishes behavior guidelines" (DeAngelis, 2006). Just as each individual is unique, so is the culture of each academic institution (Ginsberg et al., 1994). However, there are some common traits that are identified as a personality type, and there are some commonalities that differentiate employment cultures. Through an informal survey of 149 employee assistance professionals working in higher educational settings, colleges and universities, the authors identified some ubiquitous–or nearly ubiquitous–academic cultural characteristics. These cultural characteristics roughly cluster around features of all businesses: mission, flexibility, decision making and infrastructure. Along with many of the respondents, the authors, too, have had employee assistance program (EAP) experience in both academia and corporate America. The differences between corporate culture and academic culture will be contrasted across these four components. How these differences impact the delivery of employee assistance service will be explored. Finally, to advance Franz's (1991) recommendation that "people responsible for conducting it [the university's EAP] understand the university culture and are able to adapt to it," modifications that seem to be useful will be described.

This is the authors' attempt to distill their experiences. The complex realities of academic culture and being embedded in this complexity have impeded our finding many efficient and effective ways around these cultural obstacles. In working together, we have become even more aware that an intervention which works in one academic setting often is non-transferable. Thus, some of our recommendations may seem limp. It is hoped that our article will inspire other EAP professionals to build upon our recommendations, tailor them to their individual institutions, and customize service delivery accordingly. It is also hoped that our clarification will be impetus and encouragement to others to identify broadly applicable, viable procedures to assist people and their institutions.

BRIEF LITERATURE REVIEW

Mintzberg (as cited by Grosch et al., 1996), in describing academic environments as "professional bureaucracy," discussed the flexibility component. When Grosch et al. (1996) mention that "output and job performance can be troublesome to measure," they are detailing some of the infrastructure differences. Cocciarelli (1985), coordinator of one of the earliest EAPs in higher education, may have been the first to write about the difficulties of confronting alcohol abuse in an academic infrastructure. Like Baxter (1988), Dugan (1989), Roberts-DeGennaro (1989), and Harlacher and Goodman (1991) before him, Bean (1993) pointedly elaborates on the problems that academic infrastructure creates. Most of these authors are talking about tenured faculty; very few mention how this cultural component impacts the staff side of academia. Throughout their article, Balgopal and Stollak (1992) delineate aspects of academic culture which match one or more of the four components. Many of the points they make are similar to the observations and suggestions to be made in this paper. As this quick review demonstrates, each of the four components has been identified previously. However, all four have not been considered together as interlocking facets of academic culture.

MISSION

In order to compare the mission of educational institutions to corporate America it is important to identify the elements of a mission statement. These are the building blocks of the organization. Thus, the mission: (a) identifies a common purpose for the organization; (b) defines the scope of services and/or products of the organization; (c) describes the activities and the operations of the organization; and (d) creates standards of performance for the organization.

Reflected in the mission statement may be the organization's values, beliefs, behavior and practices. These create the culture of an organization. Differences between the academic culture and the corporate culture are evident in their missions.

Differences

The primary differences that set educational institutions apart from most of corporate America are in the areas of teaching, research, tenure, funding and service. These combined aspects serve to create the mission of an institution of higher education.

Teaching

Teaching is a fundamental responsibility in academia. This is highlighted, for instance, in the very first part of Stony Brook University's mission statement: "to provide comprehensive undergraduate, graduate, and professional education of the highest quality" (Stony Brook University Web site). The purpose of an educational institution to not only educate the community, but in so doing develop future professionals and leaders.

Research

Another significant responsibility of the academic mission is the pursuit and advancement of knowledge through science and research. Eugene Rice (1996) in *Making a Place for the New American Scholar* identified the academic profession through a 1974 consensus:

1. Research is the central professional endeavor and focus of academic life.
2. Quality in the profession is maintained by peer review and professional autonomy.
3. Knowledge is pursued for its own sake.
4. The pursuit of knowledge is best organized by discipline.
5. Reputations are established in national and international professional associations.
6. Professional rewards and mobility accrue to those who persistently accentuate their specialization.
7. The distinctive task of the academic professional is the pursuit of cognitive truth.

These two fundamental responsibilities–imparting and extending knowledge–are in contrast to the core purpose for business. Corporations are driven by competition to gain profit. Success is evaluated primarily in terms of bottom line earnings. In comparison to corporate America, the success of educational institutions is measured by: (a) the amount of research dollars generated, (b) the ranking of prestigious faculty including Nobel Prize laureates, (c) the caliber and quality of students, (d) the ranking of the university as compared to its peer institutions (e) revenues from licensed technology and (f) revenues from student enrollment.

Academic cultures, at least in theory, exist to further knowledge through research and to educate through teaching. This contrast is brought into relief by the current identity crises that some academic institutions face. They are attempting to retain or re-define these standards as their administrations move toward business models (G. Edwards, personal communication, February 23, 2006).

Tenure

Since one aspect of academic mission is to promote learning through teaching, retaining good teachers is important. The academic retention system, tenure, is one of the most significant differences between academic and corporate cultures. A major criterion for a faculty member's success in academia and for the opportunity to advance his or her career is to attain tenure as a rite of passage. Additional influences of tenure on academic culture will be discussed later in this article.

Funding

As compared to the corporate environment, educational institutions are either public or private non-profit organizations. There are several sources of funding that differentiate the non-profit from corporate America. While business is funded by income from the product–be it material or service–it sells, funding for academia derive from local, state and federal grants, fees from student enrollment, alumni contributions, and other philanthropic donors. The complexity of academic funding adds another cultural difference. Peter Drucker (1990) explains:

"Altogether, the non-profit executive deals with a greater variety of stakeholders and constituencies than the average business executive. The non-profit institution's relationship with its donors, for instance, is not known to business enterprises. A company's shareholders and customers have completely different expectations from [those of] donors."

Service

Another difference between institutions of higher education and corporate America is the amount and variety of programs and services these institutions make available to the community. An illustration of this is exemplified by Stony Brook University's mission statement. A part of its mission is "to provide leadership for economic growth, technology, and culture for neighboring communities and the wider geographic region." The statement also indicates the importance of "positioning the University in the global community" (Stony Brook University Web site).

Stony Brook University, like many of its peer institutions, provides educational opportunities for the community through the President's and Provost's lecture series; cultural events in the arts, music and theatre; mentoring programs for high school students; business development center for small business start up assistance; and technology assistance centers which partner with university researchers and local industries. A Roundtable for retired university employees facilitates their participating in the life of the university through weekly events, continuing education, and programs. In addition, the University encourages community service by sponsoring the building of local Habitant for Humanity homes and by providing a day for employees to meet with legislators at the state capital to address issues that affect education, the environment and the community. Almost all institutions of higher education make similar contributions to their surrounding communities.

Impact

The impact of the academic mission on employee assistance program (EAP) practice presents challenges particularly in terms of addressing such workplace issues as job stress, productivity, teamwork, communication, supervision and conflict. In this academic culture which often symbolizes freedom, autonomy, creativity, idea sharing and innovation faculty do not often perceive themselves as employees. Instead, they operate like small business enclaves, setting their own hours and their own performance expectations. Peter Drucker (1990) points out in his classic book, *Managing the Non-Profit Organization*, "People work in non-profits because they believe in the cause."

Depending on job classification–faculty or staff–there is, frequently, a double standard in terms of how employees are treated. The unpredictable treatment creates a climate of mistrust and fear. It also damages employee morale and erodes any sense of community. Although a double standard exists in American businesses, it is more prevalent in higher educational settings.

In addition, unionization, collegiality, in-group protectiveness, peer evaluation, and academic freedom make peer referrals [to the EAP] extremely unlikely. "In the transition from the hierarchal structure of business and industry to the less well-defined structure of higher education there appears to be more enabling of [a faculty] employee's behavior by often viewing it as the 'eccentric' or an absent-minded professor. Though these traits may be looked upon negatively by business and industry, they are often viewed as acceptable, even expected, within academia" (Bean, 1993).

Adaptation

Given the mission of institutions of higher education, some guidelines for adaptation of EAP practice are: (a) Develop relationships which will assist in workplace interventions; (b) accept that the educational mission is to be of service to various groups: students, community, donors and alumni; (c) be patient, yet persistent, with the process of organizational change and adaptation of new practices to assist impaired faculty and staff; (d) adjust–not lower–expectations: realize that there may not always be continuity and consistency in how personnel problems are addressed; (e) and implement specific marketing strategies targeting faculty, staff and their families about EAP services.

FLEXIBILITY

Differences

When comparing educational institutions and corporate America, flexibility often stands out as a significant difference. Flexibility seems more valued in educational settings than in their corporate counterparts. This flexibility takes on the form of creativity, individuality and diversity.

Premium On Creativity

Many people choose academia as a career path as opposed to the business sector for the flexibility which comes to them in the form of creativity. Professors, researchers and post-doctorate researchers, are encouraged to "reach higher" through imagination and originality. Not only does the academic environment foster this innovation, but it also actually protects the people who generate it. Never is this more dominant than in the tenant of "academic freedom." Academicians have an inalienable right to express themselves in the name of academic pursuits (Rice, 1996). This can take the form of extremely controversial or politically incorrect comments, and, yet, it can be a vehicle for tremendous creativity.

In the business sector, researchers are beholden to a board of trustees, stockholders and others who control the coffers. In this corporate world, an exciting project can be moving along, yet, within a day, it can be taken away or aborted for monetary or even political reasons. Conversely, educational institutions receive money from outside sources in the form of grants, endowments, even fund-raising. Oftentimes written into the grant is the expectation that the professor/researcher has final control of the project.

In academia, there are means to receive money from several funding sources, to collaborate within two or more departments for financial or academic contributions, and to have input into the policies, procedures and initiatives that run a particular department. Most corporate employers tend to streamline funding sources, minimize alliances and relationships, and give employees little to no say over organizational issues.

For non-teaching staff members in institutions of higher education, the perception of creativity can go either way. Some employees find there is little creativity in their jobs, while others experience that the overall environment of the institution allows for creative expression. Sometimes this takes the form of how one manages his or her day, how one approaches a project, or how one manages subordinates. Many colleges and universities offer classes specially designed for employees. These are often scheduled during lunch hours, and, thus, permit and encourage employees to seek creative outlets through professional development.

INDIVIDUALITY AND DIVERSITY

A second major distinction between American corporations and institutions of higher learning is the value which is placed on individuality and diversity throughout academia. The university attracts a broad range of people, who not only come from different backgrounds (ethnically, culturally), but who also actually challenge ways of thinking. Academic culture tends to encourage independent thinking, teaching and research. Glen Edwards, an EAP consultant and clinical psychologist with extensive experience in both university and corporate settings, states, "The norm in the academic world is to be unique and not fit in with the status quo but to think beyond" (personal communication, February 23, 2006). In contrast, corporate America relies on like-minded thinking and often dismisses or discourages the notion of "thinking outside the box." The academic world provides a wide variety of diversity–people, occupations, learning and opportunities–to its employees. This variety presents a constant challenge that is personally and intellectually stimulating. Deborah Haliczer of Northern Illinois University states, "The academic workplace is one with less demand for conformity, and more acceptances of individuals' work styles or lifestyles" (personal communication, February 12, 2006). It is difficult to find this range in any other setting. Generally, it does not exist outside of educational institutions.

Impact

As EAP professionals, understanding the value university clients place on flexibility is paramount. Many faculty, researchers and post-doctorate fellows choose their careers based on this value. When clients perceive lack of flexibility, when it seems to be taken away, or when there is infringement upon it, the EAP professional should understand the loss and confusion that may be felt. Simply stated, the situation may become a crisis of sorts. Obvious reactions by the client may include anger, depression, self-doubt, entitlement, loss and devaluation. The employee assistance professional more quickly empathizes with these clients–as opposed to pathologizing them–by remembering that faculty members and researchers are accustomed to flexibility and have often made conscious career choices which incorporate it.

Adaptation

As stated earlier, many academicians, as well as non-teaching employees, choose or pursue a career in the educational system based on the assumption that flexibility–in the form of creativity, individuality and diversity–is a given. The employee assistance professional needs to understand this assumption and to realize there may be a gap between rhetoric and reality. Helping clients to explore these two layers is necessary when working in the academic world. Along with this potential gap between reality and an unspoken expectation of flexibility, are the reactions of anger or loss that may occur when flexibility is lost. The employee assistance professional needs to help clients balance these contradictions. EAP professionals must carefully listen to the expectation or entitlement academicians may feel with regard to flexibility, and then help clients understand and deal with loss if their flexibility changes or does not come to fruition.

DECISION-MAKING

Though the flexible work environment in academia allows individuals to be unconventional, the decision making process is more conservative.

Differences

In comparing the decision-making processes of educational institutions with those of corporate America, we see three major distinctions: (a) the people who influence the decisions, (b) the number of people involved in making decisions, and (c) the speed with which these people make and implement decisions.

The People Who Influence The Decisions

One of the most distinctive differences between educational and corporate cultures is the people who influence decisions. University presidents, who are typically focused on public relations and fund-raising, have much less influence than do CEOs, who are more operations-oriented.

Faculty members, on the other hand, often have a tremendous amount of influence in the academic setting. For example, in some universities, faculty have successfully lobbied for, and received, their own set of policies, procedures and employee benefits. One director of a Faculty and Staff Assistance Program goes so far as to say that "faculty have joint governance in universities. There is no parallel in corporations and [this] changes the culture completely" (S. Harvey, personal communication, February 13, 2006).

Department chairpersons also have some influence in organizational decisions, like middle managers in a corporation. In contrast, however, is the unique aspect of the department chairs' roles: they are often "in place for a fixed amount of time, only to be replaced by one of their colleagues who is now their boss. What other workplace has this arrangement?" (T. Ruggieri, personal communication, February 13, 2006) Because of this role reversing, decisions that have been put into place by the former department chair may be overridden by the new one. Tom Ruggieri, the coordinator of the Faculty and Staff Assistance Program at University of Maryland, College Park, points out that "while encouraging a greater degree of fairness, it is not always the most efficient way to get things done" (personal communication, February 13, 2006).

THE NUMBER OF PEOPLE INVOLVED: COMMITTEE VERSUS CENTRALIZED DECISION-MAKER

A second major distinction between the two settings relates to the number of people involved in making decisions. In academia, committees drive most decisions. In a culture that values independent thinking and deliberation, it is no surprise that decisions usually involve participation at many levels. Often decisions only go forward when there is consensus. According to one EAP consultant, "Academic cultures seem to operate more on a consensus-based model where outcome is decided by many stakeholders. Information is gathered and processed and presented and re-processed and eventually decisions are made" (G. Edwards, personal communication, February 23, 2006). Because decisions in a university setting involve more participant groups, these groups create checks and balances. The downside of having more participants, however, is that consensus is harder to reach. Sometimes, in the absence of consensus, groups fail to come to decisions. In the corporate setting, by contrast, the decision-making process is more centralized. Executives, rather than committees, make decisions; or fewer individuals are involved, so consensus is easier to reach. In some cases, a single individual makes a decision. Furthermore, since corporate decisions are typically evaluated based on profit after they are made, approval also occurs later in the process. Edwards concurs by pointing out that, in the corporate setting, accountability to shareholders and to the board is often "after the fact, almost in reverse to the way it is done in the academic world" (personal communication, February 23, 2006).

THE SPEED WITH WHICH DECISIONS ARE MADE AND IMPLEMENTED

Because of the committee-driven aspect of academic culture, groups make decisions at a much slower pace than in the private sector. Furthermore, once decisions are finally made in academia, their implementation seems to occur at a very slow pace. Delays can result from the very qualities that are valued in academic culture: independent thinking and questioning of authority. Although these qualities enrich university life in many ways, they also can pose barriers to employees' acceptance of change. Such barriers impede timely compliance with new policies, procedures, and other campus initiatives. Some observers assert that the university environment is resistant to change and is not open to experimentation. Dr. John DiBiaggio, in an interview with Claudio Sanchez, said, "Universities don't like to change dramatically. They're very traditional places. Some would even say that they're rigid" (NPR, Morning Edition, 2/22/06).

Impact

It is important for EAP professionals to realize that that they need buy-in from those groups and individuals who influence decisions within the organization, including faculty and chair people. Also, since decisions are driven by committees in academia, it is important for EAP professionals to be aware of the need for consensus. Accordingly, EAPs and their managers should expect the decision-making process to move slowly, particularly when it involves recommendations for departmental changes or termination of employees, especially faculty. Along these lines, EAP professionals should understand that management may have less leverage when they consult about faculty behavior than corporate management has when consulting about employees. EAPs in an academic setting should expect to encounter delay when attempting to coordinate employee or supervisory education, cultural change, or organizational change.

Adaptation

As discussed, decisions in academia are rarely made without debate and participation at many levels. Because of this, it is important for EAP professionals to gather wide support. One way of doing this is by establishing an EAP advisory board that includes faculty, department chairs, members of Human Resources, and others who influence decisions within the organization. When recommending policy changes, it is a good idea to gather evidence, ask key individuals and groups for input, and allow time for review. Since these processes move slowly in a university setting, it is necessary for EAP professionals to have patience and encourage managers to do the same. For example, when faced with contentious situations such as employee misconduct or discrimination allegations, EAPs should encourage managers to document thoroughly and consult with the powers-that-be within the university, such as Human Resources, General Counsel, and EEO offices, rather than acting hastily on their own.

Getting the input of influential decision-makers not only can help with buy-in, but can also provide support for the EAP itself. Because faculty members have such an influence in the organization, it is recommended that employee assistance professionals find ways of initiating contact with faculty and gaining their support. Some ideas include conducting outreach meetings, including EAP materials in new-hire packets for faculty, joining professional faculty groups, and presenting at faculty meetings and chairpersons' retreats. The changes that take place in the university setting will usually be small ones, but by gathering wide support, reaching out to faculty and chairpersons, and having patience and persistence, a university EAP will have a greater chance of success.

INFRASTRUCTURE

All EAP professionals need to be aware of how an organization is structured internally. The key components in defining an employer's infrastructure are: the people who make the decisions, the personnel policies which are in place, the people who are responsible for enforcing policies, and the way in which employees are held accountable for adhering to the institution's (or a subset's) policies. In this section some differences between the internal structures of corporate and educational entities will be sketched along with some of the implications and recommendations for an EAP professional in an academic setting.

Differences

In a corporate entity it is generally clear who is the managerial staff and who is the front-line worker, the one responsible for producing the product or service. However, in an academic setting, the traditional "corporate hierarchy" represented by a simple organizational chart is rare. Generally, a hierarchical chart can not portray the many independent units that operate under a larger university umbrella. Consequently, there are many ramifications when it comes to management and personnel practices.

Policies

It is important to clarify that policies of an academic institution on a campus-wide basis may be more guidelines than practice rules. In contrast, in a business entity there is one set of policies and procedures. While an academic setting often has policies for the entire institution, many departments within that setting have their own variations. These may be more structured or more flexible. However, when managing their work forces, departments are like silos with independent ways of handling personnel issues.

Perception Of Status

In academic settings there are many more differences in status that are identifiable. Because a person's perception of status impacts upon his or her morale, there was a movement in the last decade by corporate employers to provide some increased status for their employees by labeling them "associates." As mentioned earlier, in universities there are those who see themselves as professionals in their chosen field and not as employees at all (Rice, 1996). Even some unionized staff consider themselves members of their "professions" (i.e., Trades Member, etc.). There are others, though, who identify themselves as employees: support, administrative, and maintenance staff.

Unsupervised Employees

The largest manifest difference is that in academia there is a larger number of employees who are not supervised in a traditional hierarchical model: most notably the instructional staff. In traditional corporate settings most employees can be located on an organizational chart reporting directly to a supervisor. In contrast in academia, there is a wide mix of reporting formats.

Many from the International Association of Employee Assistance Professionals in Education (IAEAPE) membership have reported that up to half of their "employee" base is instructional. These teachers are not supervised in a traditional one-on-one manner at all. Supervision of instructional staff may be by a one time observation of their instruction or by student evaluations. Those pursuing tenure in academia are most likely under review by a team of colleagues, not one supervisor. In this instance, a tenure-track instructor could be reviewed by all of his or her tenured colleagues for years. She or he would need to please each member of the tenure review committee. Once tenured, many instructors are likely to believe they do not need any more supervision. Once tenured, they may only be chastised for infractions such as embarrassment to their profession. Similar to instructors, research staff also may not be directly supervised. To keep their positions, they need to maintain their grant flow. As long as the grants flow, many conduct issues are ignored.

Most other employees in academia–administrative support staff, service staff–report via traditional hierarchical models. They have performance and conduct expectations similar to their equivalents in the business sector.

Impact

As suggested before, in academic settings discipline and conduct standards are more varied. Since most of the faculty do not consider themselves employees, they do not hold themselves accountable to performance measures. Setting performance or work plans for instructional staff is unlikely. In a *Chronicle Careers* article, "Discipline and Punish," Stanley Fish (2002) notes "faculty is naturally responsible and will continue to be so as long as it remains free to do whatever it likes". Thus the concepts of accountability and of discipline are remote. Fish also describes the bottom line for disciplining faculty: "You have to have falsified your credentials or been convicted of or admitted to, a felony or have disappeared from the scene of teaching entirely or have manufactured and sold a controlled substance or physically assaulted a member of the university community or engaged in sexual misconduct so egregious that you are likely to go to jail anyway. And even if there is evidence that you have done one of these things, you are protected against hasty judgment by procedures so elaborate and time consuming that the appropriate officials in your university will either be reluctant to set them in motion or fail to execute them properly." Note there is nothing at all in that statement about the level of performance.

This belief by faculty that they are retained for what they know, not what they do often permeates to other professional employee groups. In the *Making a Place for the New American Scholar,* Eugene Rice (1996) noted that "quality in the profession is maintained by peer review and professional autonomy." Some instructional staff believe that there is no need for them to be supervised at all, or that no one has the right to supervise or hold them accountable. In "Faculty Misconduct and Discipline," Donna Euben, AAUP Staff Counsel, and Barbara Lee note that "a system of 'progressive discipline' has emerged that is standard practice in most of these [nonacademic] organizations" (2005, Introduction section). They go on to note, though, that this is rare for faculty.

So how are faculty issues addressed? Euben and Lee state that "depending on the seriousness of the allegations, a chair or dean *might* [italics added] create an ad-hoc faculty committee to review the allegations and to make findings of whether or not misconduct occurred and to recommend what type of sanction to impose" (2005, Policies for faculty discipline section). Again, there is no reference to performance. A committee is considering the matter. The behavior of academics is judged acceptable or unacceptable by their peers not by someone to whom they report. As discussed in the decision making section of the article, deans and chairpersons may be in their positions for short periods of time and on a rotating schedule. Thus, it is possible that the committee who is considering conduct concerns includes someone who is the problem person's boss today, but might be supervised by that problem person in the near future. Committee members who are evaluating the behavior of a faculty member may be compromised or have conflicts of interest.

Several employee assistance professionals have attested to this phenomenon. Deborah Haliczer, Director of Employee Relations at the Northern Illinois University, writes, "faculty and other professional staff measure their performance by profession-based standards and not always necessarily against colleagues in their department" (D. Haliczer, personal communication, February 13, 2006). Tom Ruggieri of the University of Maryland states "certainly [they] have people in charge but usually not in the way that a traditional CEO is in charge" (T. Ruggieri, personal communication, February 13, 2006). As Polly Moutevelis-Burgess, Director of the EAP for the University of Maine, states about tenure "no other setting guarantees work for life" (P. Moutevelis-Burgess, personal communication, February 15, 2006). Similar to decision making which in academic settings it is done by consensus, faculty conduct and performance are often addressed through consensual processes.

IMPLICATIONS AND RECOMMENDATIONS

In recognition of the above differences, there are some serious implications for the EAP professional. EAPs may be called upon to provide consultation and recommendations to those struggling with instructional staff behavior problems, or the behavior of others who either believe they are not to be supervised or are not subject to performance or conduct standards. The following suggestions deal with consulting to management about confronting or approaching a faculty member or "non-supervised" employee who has conduct or performance issues.

1. Explore realistic sanctions and incentives to address those unacceptable behaviors.
2. Be aware that those to whom you are consulting may not accept the practicality of changing behavior by enforcing consequences.
3. Make specific suggestions such as: (a) take away teaching assignments, (b) take away graduate assistants, (c) assign to research only, (d) reduce or eliminate support staff, (e) remove from committee assignments (which may reduce status), or (f) stop the tenure clock.

Euben and Lee continue this list with some other options:

1. Refer the person of concern to a committee for review.
2. Start "de-tenure" proceedings.
3. Explore demotion in rank or class monitoring.
4. Institute sanctions: oral or written reprimand, restitution, apologies, suspension of merit increase, a fine, or reduction in salary for a given time (2005, Types of faculty discipline section).

In mentioning the above suggestions, the EAP professional is providing ideas for incentives and sanctions that may motivate the problem person to either change behavior or be receptive to a referral to the EAP. In addition, the employee assistance professional may advocate coaching services or wellness assistance. Above all, as noted earlier in this article, the EAP consultant in academia will have to be more patient, educate more about enabling behaviors, and suggest intervention steps earlier than he or she would in corporate America.

CONCLUSION

Academic culture is complex; some EAP interventions that work in the corporate sector are not as effective in academia. The complicating realities of academe's culture–its mission, flexibility, decision-making and infrastructure–have resulted in employee assistance professionals' fine-tuning their skills. A few of the lessons learned by providing employee assistance services to academic institutions are discussed in this paper. They are: (a) Funding sources influence decision-making, policies, and personnel practices; (b) Diversity is prevalent throughout the institution–in the staff and the faculty; (c) The expectation of institutional flexibility can be problematic; (d) Academic decision making is a cumbersome and slow process; and (e) Differences exist between the personnel policies and practices for instructional and non-instructional employees. Just as no two corporations are alike, no two academic settings are alike, and no two EAPs the same. Each has its unique culture and its unique responses to the personalities that make up that culture. In academic settings, as in the business sector, EAPs maximize their effectiveness by being aware of unique cultural characteristics and by customizing service delivery accordingly.

REFERENCES

Balgopal, P. R. & Stollak, M. J. (1992). Employee assistance programs: Implications for higher education. *Employee Assistance Quarterly, 7*(4), 101-118.

Baxter, A. K. (1988, February). Intervene if you dare: Reaching the "protected" academician. *The Almacan*, 13-16.

Bean, J. H. (1993, January/February). Innovations in outreach strategies with impaired faculty. *EAP Digest*, 34-37.

Cocciarelli, S. (1985). Alcoholism: Academics, academe. *The Journal(CUPA), 36*, 1-8.

DeAngelis, T. (2006). Getting to know you. *American Psychological Association Monitor on Psychology, 37,* 52-54.

Drucker, P. F. (1990). *Managing the non-profit organization: Practices and principles.* New York: HarperBusiness.

Dugan, P. (1989, July/August). Peer intervention in higher education. *EAP Digest*, 47-53.

Euben, D. R. & Lee, B. (2005, February). Faculty misconduct and discipline. Paper presented at the National Conference on Law and Higher Education, Gulfport, FL. (Retrieved on March 22, 2006, from http://www.aaup.org/Legal/info%20outlines/05legmiscon.htm).

Fish, S. (2002, November 15). Discipline and punish. *Chronicle Careers.* (Retrieved on March 20, 2006, from http://chronicle.com/jobs/2002/11/2002111501c.htm).

Franz, J. P. (1991, September/October). Developing university EAPs: A planned change perspective. *EAP Digest*, 24-29, 64.

Ginsberg, M. R., Kilburg, R. R., & Gomes, P. G. (1994, August). Integrated human services and EAPs: The Johns Hopkins experience. *EAPA Exchange*, 8-10.

Grosch, J. W., Duffy, K. G., & Hessink, T. K. (1996). Employee assistance programs in higher education: Factors associated with program usage and effectiveness. *Employee Assistance Quarterly, 11*(4), 43-57.

Harlacher, E. L. & Goodman, J. S. (1991, September/October). Social issues and EAPs in community colleges. *EAP Digest*, 30-35, 64.

National Public Radio. (2006, February 22). Failure to court faculty dooms Harvard president.*(Retrieved February 23, 2006, from* http://www.npr.org/templates/story/story.php?storyId=5227723)

Rice, R. E. (1996). *Making a place for the new American scholar.* Washington, DC: American Association for Higher Education.

Roberts-DeGennaro, M. (1989). Needs assessment for a university-based employee assistance program. *Employee Assistance Quarterly, 4*(3), 11-25.

Stony Brook University has a five-part mission. Stony Brook University Web site (Retrieved April 21, 2006, from http://www.stonybrook.edu/pres/mission.shtml)

doi:10.1300/J490v22n03_02

University Based Employee Assistance Programs and Outsourcing: The Case for Diversified Function

Daniel Hughes

SUMMARY. Academic organizations are unique settings for employee assistance practice. Recent changes in both the workplace and the employee assistance field have raised questions about the economic viability of internal university based programs. Data collected by the International Association of Employee Assistance Programs in Education (IAEAPE) indicates that a trend toward outsourcing has emerged. This paper submits a three-part strategy for university based programs to strengthen their fiscal base and reduce the risk of outsourcing. Operationally, it suggests that academically oriented programs should embrace a "Diversified Function Model" that includes the development of external contracts, practice-based research and teaching. The author argues that internal university based programs are ideally positioned to rebuild the once vigorous relationship between the employee assistance field and the academic community. The multi-faceted value of university based programs is discussed in terms of knowledge building, education and professional credibility. Accordingly, the paper concludes that university based internal programs constitute a vital resource to the field and should be maintained.
doi:10.1300/J490v22n03_03 *[Article copies available for a fee from The Haworth Document Delivery Service: 1-800-HAWORTH. E-mail address: <docdelivery@haworthpress.com> Website: <http://www.HaworthPress.com>*

[Haworth co-indexing entry note]: "University Based Employee Assistance Programs and Outsourcing: The Case for Diversified Function." Hughes, Daniel. Co-published simultaneously in *Journal of Workplace Behavioral Health* (The Haworth Press, Inc.) Vol. 22, No. 2/3, 2006/2007, pp. 27-41; and: *Employee Assistance Programs in Higher Education* (ed: R. Paul Maiden and Sally B. Philips) The Haworth Press, 2006/2007, pp. 27-41. Single or multiple copies of this article are available for a fee from The Haworth Document Delivery Service [1-800-HAWORTH, 9:00 a.m. - 5:00 p.m. (EST). E-mail address: docdelivery@haworthpress.com].

Available online at http://jwbh.haworthpress.com

doi:10.1300/J490v22n03_03

KEYWORDS. University, Employee Assistance Programs, outsourcing, knowledge building, education

INTRODUCTION

Academic organizations create unique environments for employee assistance practice. Schools, colleges, universities and teaching hospitals are simultaneously both workplaces and centers for education and research. They are occupationally stratified and tend to be organizationally decentralized. For example, universities employ diverse groups of workers from food and building service personnel to administrators and research faculty. Their internal structure is frequently composed of loosely affiliated schools, departments, divisions and educational programs, representing various academic disciplines and/or organizational functions. Most academic institutions operate on a not for profit basis and are funded by tuition, fees, grants, contracts, endowments and other forms of subsidy. The occupational culture of these institutions is distinct from other work organizations and reflects specific values, norms and conditions of employment ranging from hourly wages to academic tenure. Interestingly, the specialized nature of EAP practice in academic settings has led to the establishment of a self-select professional association called the International Association of Employee Assistance Programs in Education (IAEAPE). As a voluntary professional association, IAEAPE was organized to address occupational issues of mutual concern to its membership. The group was established in 1993 and is composed primarily of internal EAP practitioners.[1] Recent changes in both the workplace and the field of employee assistance practice have led to growing pressure on these programs. Specifically, economic restructuring, technological innovation and shifting managerial paradigms have led to a trend toward outsourcing and in some extreme cases program closings.[2] Survey data indicates that employee assistance programs are among the most frequently 'outsourced' of human resource services (The Bureau of National Affairs [BNA], 2003).

Like other sectors of the American Workplace (i.e., manufacturing, utilities, transportation etc.), academic institutions have embraced the value of employee assistance programs. During the 1970s, several university based employee assistance programs were established as the EAP movement gained increased acceptance throughout the workplace (Blum et al., 1992). These included programs at the University of Delaware, the University of Missouri and Rutgers University. Historically, the process of employee assistance program diffusion received both funding and political support from the National Institute of Alcohol Abuse and Alcoholism (NIAAA). This included a grant to the University of Missouri for a series of EAP focused conferences beginning in 1976. By 1979 57% (fifty seven percent) of all Fortune 500 companies had some form of an EAP (Roman, 1979). Initially, "the prototypical EAP" was an internal program staffed by employees of the host work organization (Roman, 1990). However, external programs would become increasingly popular, representing an alternative model of service. In these external programs EAP services were contractually negotiated and provided by outside vendors. Significantly, EAPs began to address a diverse range of problems affecting employee performance beyond the single issue of alcohol abuse (Googins, 1993). These 'broad brush' programs were quickly embraced by organizations, managers and employees as the pace of EAP diffusion accelerated throughout the 1980s and 1990s (White & Sharar, 2003). Academic institutions followed this trend frequently opting for the establishment of internal programs. However, sweeping social changes including technological innovation, the reorganization of work and economic globalization have led to profound changes in the American Workplace. Today universities and other academic institutions are implementing various techniques and business strategies from distance learning to outsourcing, as they seek to thrive in an increasingly competitive economic environment. Consequently, if internal programs are to survive in academic institutions, they must develop and implement strategies designed to sustain their existence and affirm their unique value. This paper will explore the impact of these processes, offer some concrete suggestions to strengthen internal programs in academic settings and submit an argument why these programs should be maintained and enhanced.

RISK REDUCTION STRATEGIES

The following discussion is based largely on the author's professional experience managing an internal program in an academic health care institution in New York City. Broadly, it will suggest a three-part business strategy to reduce the risk of being out-sourced including the development of external contracts, practice-based research and teaching. Additionally, the paper will discuss a number of pragmatic suggestions used to build the value of internal programs and to enhance the level of EAP organizational integration. Specifically, it will submit a 'diversified function model' for EAP practice in academic settings. However, it should be noted that, each academic institution presents its own unique challenges and opportunities. Accordingly, each program exists in a specific environment shaped by particular organizational dynamics, social histories and resources (i.e., budgets, revenues, staff skill-sets etc.). Consequently, this paper will not offer a "how to" plan but rather discuss some ideas that should assist organizational stakeholders to develop both a strategy and a rationale for the continuation of internal EAP services in academic institutions.

External Contracts

During the 1990s the American Health Care Industry was beset by waves of organizational re-engineering, decreased levels of governmental support and reduced revenues driven by the impact of managed care. Academic health care institutions were particularly vulnerable to these trends, due to the relatively high costs of medical education and technological innovation. Cumulatively, these factors led to fiscal distress in the health care industry and economic retrenchment. In recent years, both public and private universities have experienced similar fiscal constraints. Accordingly, many organizational functions, including EAP services, were reevaluated. Outsourcing was presented as an effective mechanism to reduce operating expenses. Fundamentally, this process was driven by organizational efforts to cut costs. Many internal programs were asked to justify their operating budgets. Those that couldn't were either closed or contracted out. Alternatively, some EAPs sought creative ways to generate revenue and reduce costs. As a result, several internal programs have developed 'hybrid models.' These programs have continued to provide services to their host organizations while developing accounts with external client organizations, thus generating supplemental sources of revenue. Academic health care institutions such as Partners Health Care System in Boston, the University of Maryland's School of Medicine in Baltimore and New York's Mount Sinai Medical Center have employed this model with good results. Similarly, a number of university based internal programs have found this approach useful. Unfortunately, external contracts do not always protect internal EAPs, as illustrated by the case of Continuum Health Care in New York City, which closed its program in 2001, despite multiple external contracts.[3] However, the adoption of the hybrid model usually serves to strengthen the economic base of internal programs and should be considered as a first line of defense against either program closure or outsourcing.

Research

A second strategy that has the potential to generate revenue, enhance program credibility and increase organizational integration is research. In 1995 the author presented a paper to the annual conference of the Employee Assistance Professionals Association (EAPA) entitled, "Reasons and Resources." In this paper he argued that, internal programs in academic institutions had an opportunity to expand their practice model to include research, which could potentially contribute to the knowledge base of the EA profession and generate additional program revenue. Since research activities tend to generate technology transfers that bring new ideas and techniques into research oriented programs and organizations, it was suggested that universities and academic health care institutions would be more likely to embrace both the concept and value of EAP research. Moreover, research would be perceived as consistent with one of their primary organizational missions, namely, knowledge building. Thus, applied research would offer the capacity to increase the status and credibility of an internal EAP situated within an academic environment. On one level, fundable research provides the EAP with a supplemental source of revenue. On another, it gives the program an additional source of 'cultural capital,' (Bourdieu, 1980) that could be drawn upon during critical periods of economic austerity and organizational uncertainty. However, to achieve and implement this expanded model of practice, most EAP practitioners would have to acquire additional skills. Specifically, HR and clinical acumen would need to be enhanced to include analytic and research expertise. Pragmatically, this could be achieved through various forms of professional development, such as, continuing education, mentoring relationships and by developing partnerships with established centers of workplace research.

Accordingly, the Mt Sinai EAP established a series of partnerships with centers of workplace research including, the University of Michigan's Institute of Labor and Industrial Relations, Boston University's School of Social Work, Boston College's Center for Work and Family and the ISA, Associates of Alexandria Virginia. As a consequence, the staff of the Mt Sinai Medical Center's EAP was able to work collaboratively with professional researchers. Progress was slow since the staff needed time to adjust to the demands of new tasks and responsibilities. A modest amount of program resources were allocated for technical assistance in an effort to accelerate the learning process. Gradually, the program embraced the paradigm and began to promote its new capability within the medical center. In this fashion, the programs staff were able to acquire practice based research skills through experiential learning. Hence, the Mt. Sinai EAP participated in several publicly and privately funded research projects. Eventually, these efforts led to the development of a study designed to test the feasibility and efficacy of providing long term counseling services to high-risk clients (Hughes et al., 2004). This project served as a concrete example of the program's newly acquired ability to develop and implement a research project from proposal writing through publication (Hughes et al., 2004). It also served to enhance the program's credibility within the context of an academic health care center.

Teaching

The third proposed strategy to assist academic EAPs, to increase their organizational value and avoid out-sourcing, involves staff appointment to the teaching faculty. EAP involvement in the educational mission of academic organizations is consistent with the institutional objectives of schools, colleges and universities. Most EAP practitioners employed in academic settings hold graduate level credentials. Many are involved in the supervision and training of graduate students placed in their programs. Therefore, it is strongly suggested that, EAP staff working in academic settings should pursue faculty appointments. This is particularly useful in universities offering professional programs in EAP related disciplines such as psychology, counseling, social work, management and industrial relations to name a few. This important extension of EAP function supports professional development and simultaneously works to increase the program's organizational value. Faculty appointments serve to enhance both the EAP and its staff in many important ways. First, they help employee assistance practitioners to expand and strengthen their skills. Secondly, faculty appointments create opportunities for EAP practitioners to build collegial relationships with important program stakeholders within the organization including other faculty, departmental chairs, academic deans and provosts. These relationships have the potential to increase program utilization by improving the level of EAP/Organizational integration. Thirdly, EAP faculty membership supports the notion that, these particular internal programs are staffed with professionally trained specialists, who are intimately familiar with the culture of academic organizations. Clearly, lecturing is a value-added activity that can be quantified and used to garner additional institutional support for program operations. Moreover, teaching serves as a logical complement to practice-based research activities. Accordingly, teaching and research become two sides of the same academic coin.

A three part business strategy employing the development of external contracts, practice-based research and teaching activities provides the internal EAP, situated in an academic setting, with an enhanced resource base. This is achieved through a diversification of EAP function to include research and teaching. Clearly, many EAPs have diversified their service packages to include elements such as work/life and wellness services. However, few programs have diversified their functions in the manner suggested in this discussion. As a business strategy the 'diversified function model' allows the EAP flexibility and protection from unanticipated events such as fiscal contractions. For example, the loss of an external contract can be offset by the acquisition of a research grant. Support from colleagues on the faculty can be critical during times of fiscal constraint, program re-evaluation and organizational restructuring. Similarly, resources generated by these activities can significantly reduce the 'on budget cost' of program operations, making it a less attractive target for outsourcing. However, it should be noted that all successful EAPs (internal, external or hybrid) are based on solid, carefully constructed professional relationships. The key to success is to use this particular strategy to strengthen programmatic support, enhance organizational integration and affirm the role of employee assistance practice as a valuable form of 'knowledge work' (Reich, 2001).

Generally, the suggested three-part strategy will help align the EAP with the business model of most academic institutions and will strengthen its economic power base. The 'Diversified Function Model' of EAP practice should emphasize the program's administrative, clinical, research and educational dimensions. It is suggested that such a program be situated within an organizational matrix that connects the organization's Human Resource Department with the research and educational functions of an academic institution. Operationally, the EAPs' organizational and clinical activities are directed toward the resolution of performance and productivity problems. This is accomplished through the application of EAP Core Technology (Roman & Blum, 1985) and serves a human resource function. Similar services are provided to the program's external clients as a revenue generating activity. The program's research and educational activities are designed to reflect and support the mission of the contemporary research university or academic health care institution. Hence, the operational paradigm of a "diversified function"

EAP includes direct services, research and teaching and should replicate the business model of its' host organization.

A few basic suggestions will help those inclined to explore the potential of this expanded model of EAP practice. Many of these recommendations are equally relevant to other settings of internal EAP practice, while some are specific to academic institutions. First, take the time to know your organization. Pay attention to the details. Use the technique of participant observation to learn and understand the culture of your workplace. Identify potential problems such as inter-departmental boundary disputes. Clearly delineate the parameters of EAP practice and distinguish them other organizational services. Form partnerships and avoid turf battles wherever possible. Clearly emphasize and explain EAP policies and privacy safeguards to all clients, stakeholders and other relevant constituencies. Appreciate organizational nuances and use them to demonstrate the value of your EAP. Maximize and leverage your position as 'an insider'. Become familiar with your school or organization's mission. Understand your institution's strategic plan. Participate in its development whenever possible. Direct your program's research capability toward issues of concern to the institution such as recruitment and retention. Align the goals of your EAP to the organization's strategic plan and mission. Invest in the development of relationships with key organizational stakeholders. The importance of these relationships cannot be overemphasized. Explore and build partnerships wherever possible, especially in the area of research. Publish and promote the results of your work. Pursue academic appointments for yourself and your staff. Establish links to academic departments. Seek mentors. Join academic committees. Use research and teaching as opportunities to expand your skills and expertise. Emphasize the value of these skills and activities and promote them throughout your organization. Embrace the concept of interdisciplinary scholarship and the culture of life-long learning. Make the internal model work for you and your institution. Create a program not easily replicated by an external vendor. Lastly, use the resources generated by your activities to sustain the effort.

KNOWLEDGE BUILDING, EDUCATION AND PROFESSIONALISM

Our discussion has focused on the 'diversified function model' as a strategy that academically situated programs can use to reduce the risk of outsourcing. We must now turn our attention to explore the broader issue of why university based employee assistance programs should be maintained and protected from outsourcing. The answer to this question rests in the special and unique value these programs possess and their potential contributions to the field, specifically, in the areas of knowledge building, education and professionalism.

Historically, professional status in America emerged as a product of those sweeping social forces that transformed both the nation and its university system during the late-Nineteenth Century. Within the occupational context of the American Workplace, professional status evolved to include central themes, elements and understandings (Flexner, 1915). These included access to a specialized body of knowledge and mastery of particular practices, methods and techniques. Typically, professional status requires the completion of a prescribed program of higher education and the acquisition of specific competencies and skills. Additionally, professionals are expected to pursue advanced knowledge building and adhere to appropriate systems of values and ethics. Lastly, social legitimacy requires that the focus of professional practice be directed toward the public good (Freidson, 1986, 1988).[4] Clearly, these issues have great relevance for the contemporary employee assistance profession.

Core Technology

Since the field's inception, practitioners and researchers have sought to articulate the knowledge, methods and techniques specific to the field of employee assistance. This effort led to the articulation of a cluster of central elements known as the EAP Core Technology (Roman & Blum, 1988). These elements have been generally accepted as reflecting the central features of employee assistance practice. However, others have suggested that this core technology should be expanded to include wellness and work/life technologies (Erfurt et al., 1992; Googins, 1991). More recently, some practitioners have argued that critical incident management should be included as an element of EAP practice in the post 9/11 world (Gill et al., 2002). Cumulatively, the employee assistance profession has come to be built upon a well-developed and evolving platform of specific theory, knowledge, and practice. It is important to note that, much of the early research on the nature and efficacy of employee assistance programs was conducted by university based researchers (Trice & Roman, 1972, Googins, 1975, Erfurt & Foote, 1977, Foote et al., 1978). Their work served to enhance the credibility of the field and support the professional status of employee assistance practice through the rigorous application of scientific method. Evidence based knowledge building continues to be one of the cornerstones of professional practice. Problematically, the link between the academic community and the employee assistance profession has weakened over time. There appears to be little incentive for private sector for profit employee assistance programs to invest in university based research. However, university based EAPs, that adopt the 'diversified function model' offer the field an important opportunity to rebuild these critical relationships through the development of practice-based research partnerships.

EAPS, Education and Knowledge Building

It has been noted that, professional status presumes access to a specialized body of knowledge, frequently acquired through the completion of a program of higher education (Freidson, 1988). In 1986 the Employee Assistance Professional Association (EAPA) implemented a certification process designed to identify minimal standards and qualifications for professional practice (EAPA, 1996). The Employee Assistance Certification Commission (EACC) was established to develop and oversee the process leading to the Certified Employee Assistance Professional (CEAP) credential. Although the EACC achieved considerable success in developing a credential process, the field has not been able to reach consensual agreement on educational standards for employee assistance practice. Interestingly, a number of graduate-school programs in disciplines ranging from social work to counseling psychology have developed occupational or workplace focused sub-specialties. Unfortunately, there remains no agreement on an educational model for employee assistance education, leaving the field without clear links to graduate-level professional education. However, many internal university based employee assistance practitioners are involved in student education. Usually these practitioners hold advanced degrees and supervise students in their respective disciplines (social work, psychology etc.). Therefore, these educationally oriented programs serve a dual function, namely, as sites for experiential learning and labs for the still unfinished project of developing an EAP educational model. In order to survive, all professions must train and educate new practitioners. Problematically, when university based programs are contracted out to external vendors both jobs and field internships are usually lost. If the profession is to develop and maintain the capacity to educate its next generation, these jobs and field placements are a critical resource and should be protected. As many EAP practitioners approach retirement the field can ill afford to lose its few existing educational mechanisms.[5] Before the field decides how to train the next generation of EAP professionals it needs to consider current and future workplace trends with care (Karoly & Panis, 2004).

Within this context, it would seem, that university-based, internal EAPs are ideally positioned to make contributions to the employee assistance profession in the critical areas of knowledge building and education. Clearly, EAP practitioners in academic settings have been influenced by the special nature of their work organizations. It would seem that university based employee assistance professionals are both capable of and committed to the process of knowledge building. This is reflected by the collection of articles in the current journal. As a group, university based employee assistance professionals are multidisciplinary. They are trained in fields ranging from business administration to social work, from counseling psychology to urban anthropology. Most hold graduate level credentials, and many have trained EAP students. Accordingly, they form a professional resource which can and should be directed toward the unfinished task of developing an educational model for EAP practice. If as suggested, university based employee assistance professionals expand their professional portfolios to include academic appointments, this project will be advanced. It is unlikely that the private, for-profit sector of the EAP field could or would engage in research and educational activities of the types discussed. Significantly, professional credibility depends on the dual processes of knowledge building and education. Both knowledge building and education are central to the mission and purpose of contemporary universities. Consequently, it is on this level that a compelling argument for preserving university based internal EAPs begins to emerge.

CONCLUSION

Research and education are two fundamental elements of professional practice. In each case, they support professional legitimacy and serve to meet the public interest. Disturbingly, the pace of evidence-based EAP research has slowed over the past ten years. Illustratively, the last published systematic national survey of employee assistance programs was conducted in the early 1990s (Hartwell et al., 1994). In contrast, interest in cost-benefit and return on investment (ROI) studies continues to be strong (Attridge & Fletcher, 2000). However, the contribution of these studies to the knowledge base of the field is circumscribed by their emphasis on cost analysis and the dictates of the 'business case'. Lamentably, the once flourishing field of EAP research has diminished. Many factors have contributed to the decline of EAP related research. They include, shifting governmental funding priorities, the increasingly 'privatized' nature of the EAP field, weakened relationships with the academic research community and the lack of an accepted university based educational model for EAP training and practice. It previously appeared, during the 1980s that, graduate programs of social work would embrace the EAP movement and that occupational social work programs would offer the employee assistance field an important link to graduate level training. However, by the following decade this outcome did not materialize as social work perspectives on workplace practice grew both numerous and diffuse (Kurzman & Akabas, 1993). Accordingly, consensual agreement on an educational model for employee assistance practice continues to remain elusive. Today, there are only four theoretically diverse masters level programs in social work offering an occupational focus in the United States. Clearly, the establishment of a university based program for EAP education should become a priority for the field.

The form and function of employee assistance has changed greatly since the days of the early occupational alcoholism programs. It has been argued by some that the nature and survival of employee assistance programs should be left to the marketplace. Accordingly, each program whether internal or external would stand on its value to both investors and to client organizations measured in terms of 'return on investment' (ROI) and profitability. This market-based approach dictates that, program services and survival should be determined by economic competition. If external vendors can provide employee assistance services more efficiently, then they should prevail. This approach has lead to a practice model based on competitively negotiated contracts and commodity pricing (Sharar & Hertenstein, 2006). Unfortunately, this transformation of employee assistance practice into a menu based cluster of service/commodities sometimes referred to as, "the integrated model," has distorted the professional nature of the field.

In contrast, this paper submits that, university based employee assistance programs are an important resource that supports the professional nature of the field by enhancing its legitimacy. It offers the 'diversified function model' as both a progressive and a protective strategy. The model is progressive because it holds that, employee assistance practice is fundamentally 'knowledge work.' It addresses two issues important to the field, namely, knowledge building and education. The model is also protective because it provides university based programs a three-part strategy to support economic viability. Accordingly, university based programs have the capacity to be self-sustaining through income generating contracts for service, funded research projects and value-added activities such as teaching. Moreover, they create opportunities to rebuild research partnerships between EAP practitioners and university based scholars. The resulting synergy has the potential to strengthen universities, academic departments, work organizations and the profession while enhancing the lives of working people. In conclusion, university based employee assistance programs are special settings for employee assistance practice. They have the capacity to serve as both centers of knowledge building and professional education. As such, they should be maintained and protected from privatization.

NOTES

1. An unpublished 2003 survey of 57 colleges and universities representing a significant segment of the membership of the IAEAPE revealed that seventy seven percent (N = 44) of the respondents were internal programs.

2. The current leadership of the IAEAPE reports that three of its member organizations were 'outsourced' during 2005. These included Harvard University, New York University and Kent State.

3. Ironically, this program serviced two major hospital centers in Manhattan and was closed eleven days before the World Trade Center Attacks.

4. This is an issue that receives far too little attention among many professions. The implicit understanding (or social contract) is that the privileges associated with professional status require commensurate attention to the public benefit. Currently, the interests of organizational clients and other stakeholders disproportionately shape the nature of EA practice. The discussion is expressed within the vocabulary of business. Accordingly, effectiveness is exclusively measured in terms of return on investment. Rarely, is there any mention of the social benefits derived from addressing and resolving the problems of working people.

5. In a 2005 survey of the New York City Chapter of the Employee Assistance Professional Association (EAPA) it was found that the average age of chapter members was fifty-four (Hughes and Warley).

REFERENCES

Attridge, M., & Fletcher, L. (2000). *EAP Cost Benefit Analysis/Effectiveness*. EAPA, Inc.: Arlington VA.

Blum, T., Martin, J. & Roman, P. (1992) *A Research Note on EAP Prevalence, Components and Utilization.* Journal of Employee Assistance Research. Vol. 1, No.1, pp. 209-229.

BNA, Inc. (2003). "*HR Outsourcing: Managing Costs & Maximizing Provider Relations. Workforce Strategies.*" Volume 21, No. 11. BNA, Inc.: Washington D.C.

Bourdieu, P. (1980). *The Logic of Practice.* Stanford, California: Stanford University Press.

Employee Assistance Professional Association. (1996). *Many Parts One Purpose.* EAPA, Inc.: Arlington VA.

Erfurt, J., & Foote, A. (1977). *Occupational Employee Assistance Programs for Substance Abuse and Mental Health Problems.* ILIR Worker Health Program: Ann Arbor, MI.

Erfurt, J., Foote, A., & Heirich, M. (1991) "*Integrating Employee Assistance and Wellness: Current and Future Core Technologies of a Megabrush Program.*" Journal of Employee Assistance Research. Vol. 1, no. 1, pp. 1-31.

Flexner, A. (1915). "*Is Social Work a Profession?*" School and Society. 1 901-911.

Foote, A., Erfurt, J., Strauch, P., & Guzzardo, T. (1978). *Cost-Effectiveness of Occupational Employee Assistance Programs: Test of an evaluation method.* ILIR Worker Health Program: Ann Arbor, MI.

Freidson, E. (1986). *Professional Powers: A Study of the Institutionalization of Formal Knowledge.* Chicago: University of Chicago Press.

Freidson, E. (1988). *Profession of Medicine: A Study of the Sociology of Applied Knowledge.* Chicago: University of Chicago Press.

Gill, D., Feerst, D., Sanchez, W., Young, K., & Taylor, T. (2002) "*On the Front Lines: Vision, planning position EAPs for successful response to critical incidents.*" EAP Digest. Summer 2002.

Googins, B. (1975) "*Employee Assistance Programs.*" Social Work, 20, 464-475.

Googins, B. (1991) *Work/family Stress: Private lives-public responses.* Greenwich CT: Auburn House Press.

Googins, B. (1993). "*Work-Site Research: Challenges and Opportunities for Social Work.*" In Work and Wellbeing, Kurzman, P and Akabas, S. (eds.) Washington D.C.: NASW Press.

Hartwell T., French, M., Potter, F., Steele, P., Zarkin, G., & Rodman, N. (1994) "*Prevalence, Cost and Characteristics of Employee Assistance Programs (EAPs) in the U.S.*" Research Triangle Park, N.C. Research Triangle Institute.

Hughes, D. (1995). "*Reasons and Resources.*" Paper presented at the 24th Annual Conference, Employee Assistance Professional Association. Seattle, WA.

Hughes, D., & Warley, R. (2005). "*Research Partnerships, Horizontal Integration and Knowledge Building.*" Paper presented at the 34th Annual Conference, Employee Assistance Professional Association. Philadelphia, PA.

Hughes, D., Elkin, C., & Epstein, I. (2004). "*Long-term Counseling: A feasibility study of extended follow-up services with high-risk EAP clients.*" Journal of Employee Assistance. 1st Quarter, 2004.

Karoly, L., & Panis, C. (2004). *The 21st Century at Work: Forces Shaping the Future Workforce and Workplace in the United States.* Santa Monica CA: Rand Corporation.

Kurzman, P., & Akabas, S. (1993) *Work and Wellbeing: The Occupational Social Work Advantage.* Washington D.C.: NASW Press.

Reich, R. (2001). *The Future of Success.* New York: Alfred A. Knopf.

Roman, P. (1979). "*The emphasis on alcoholism in employee assistance programs: New perspectives on an unfinished debate.*" Labor Management Journal on Alcoholism, 9, 186-191.

Roman, P. editor. (1990). *Alcohol Problem Intervention in the Workplace.* Westport Connecticut: Quorum Books.

Roman, P. & Blum, T. (1985). "*The core technology of employee assistance programs.*" Almacan 15, 8-12.

Sharar, D., & Hertenstein, E. (2006). "*Perspectives on Commodity Pricing in Employee Assistance Programs (EAPs): A Survey of the EAP Field.*" Unpublished manuscript. Copyright WorldatWork.

Trice, H., & Roman, P. (1972). *Spirits and Demons at Work.* Ithaca NY.: ILR Press.

White, W., & Sharar, D. (2003) "*Origins, Evolution and Solutions*" EAP Digest (3): 16-24.

doi:10.1300/J490v22n03_03

Change, Evolution and Adaptation of an University EAP: Process and Outcome at The University of Saskatchewan

Rick Csiernik
David Hannah
James Pender

SUMMARY. The University of Saskatchewan EAP was instituted in 1989, however, as occurs in many EAPs that are functioning well, little additional evaluative attention was paid to the program other than the production of annual reports for the following decade and a half. However, organizational changes within the University applied additional pressure upon the EAP which led to the question of whether the original model still best served the needs of the University, its faculty and staff. A Review Panel consisting of two external consultants and a senior University administrator was struck to examine the program as the University entered its second century of providing post-secondary education. The panels' program evaluation consisted of an examination of 29 documents, an analysis of 12 Western Canadian universities, facilitation of seven focus groups (n = 48), interviewing of 19 individuals unable to attend focus group sessions, review of 13 written submissions and consultation with members of the EAP committee and University administration. The process resulted in a series of recommendations that if implemented would significantly alter the way occupational assistance

[Haworth co-indexing entry note]: "Change, Evolution and Adaptation of an University EAP: Process and Outcome at The University of Saskatchewan." Csiernik, Rick, David Hannah, and James Pender. Co-published simultaneously in *Journal of Workplace Behavioral Health* (The Haworth Press, Inc.) Vol. 22, No. 2/3, 2006/2007, pp. 43-56; and: *Employee Assistance Programs in Higher Education* (ed: R. Paul Maiden and Sally B. Philips) The Haworth Press, 2006/2007, pp. 43-56. Single or multiple copies of this article are available for a fee from The Haworth Document Delivery Service [1-800-HAWORTH, 9:00 a.m. - 5:00 p.m. (EST). E-mail address: docdelivery@haworthpress.com].

Available online at http://jwbh.haworthpress.com

doi:10.1300/J490v22n03_04

is provided at the University. This then raises the question of how often and extensively should EAPs that are meeting the goals that they were created to address be examined in the current environment of constantly evolving and changing organization structures and needs? doi:10.1300/J490v22n03_04

KEYWORDS. Program evaluation, university, Canada

INTRODUCTION

The University of Saskatchewan was founded in 1907 in Saskatoon, just two years after the creation of the province, to provide traditional and innovative post-secondary education. Its mission statement proclaims that:

> *"The University of Saskatchewan belongs to the people of Saskatchewan. As an academic community, our mission is to achieve excellence in the scholarly activities of teaching, discovering, preserving, and applying knowledge."*
>
> University of Saskatchewan, 1993

The University's goal is to provide liberal arts, professional, and applied education in preparing students to help the people of Saskatchewan build an agriculturally-based province with the economic and cultural benefits of modern urban society. As the University prepared for its second century of providing post-secondary education it undertook a significant organizational restructuring resulting in substantive actual and perceived changes throughout the entire university system including a new philosophy for the human resources division (University of Saskatchewan, 2003). Among the issues raised within this document was if the Employee Assistance Program (EAP) was meeting the needs of the evolving university structure. This question led to a formal review by a panel of two external evaluators in association with a senior member of the university administration not involved in the day-to-day operation of the EAP to:

1. review and assess services provided by the EAP according to objective evaluation standards within the EAP field;
2. assess effectiveness of the EAP against its mandate in terms of meeting current and future needs of the University and to identify an appropriate level of financial support for the program;
3. identify options and services that would provide an EAP based on best practices in the context of the University of Saskatchewan Strategic Directions; and,
4. identify an appropriate level of resources, financial, human and facilities, required to deliver and support an EAP program based on best practice for 2005 and forward.

THE UNIVERSITY OF SASKATECHEWAN EMPLOYEE ASSISTANCE PROGRAM

The University of Saskatchewan EAP was instituted in 1989 with the stated purpose of providing assessment referral and short-term counselling for any employee requesting assistance for personal issues or work related concerns, that may impair the ability of that employee to function effectively in the performance of duties. EAP services were made available to all University employees, unionized and non-unionized as well as their family members. It was constituted as a voluntary, confidential service with no mandated component though both management and union members were able to recommend to an employee or peer to use the service, though that component was never formalized in a written policy.

Since its implementation the EAP was staffed by two employees, one male with a Masters degree in Social Work who also served as Program Director since the program's initiation and a female administrative support person. The Director was responsible for assessment of client issues, short-term counselling, referral to the community for more extended counselling, program promotion and program administration along with involvement with the critical incident response team. Six multi-disciplinary private counselling agencies in the Saskatoon area were contracted to provide longer term counselling for employees and their families. External counsellors received a maximum fee per client served which fell below the average private practice rate in return for being part of the roster of recommended University EAP counsellors. This however, led to a cap of typically six sessions for most clients.

Administration of the EAP was through an Employee Assistance Board which reported to the Vice-President of Finance and Administration. No one comprehensive EAP policy was ever created rather, the policies governing the program were situated within the various collective agreements with the last substantive revision being the addition of a critical incident protocol in 1992. The University of Saskatchewan provided all financial support for operation of the EAP though the day-to-day administration of the program was the responsibility of a 12 member voluntary Administrative Board comprised of two representatives from each of the Administrative and Supervisory Personnel Association, the Canadian Union of Public Employees Locals 1975 and 3287, the University of Saskatchewan Faculty Association, the University administration along with two members external to the university, including at least one service provider. Thus, since its beginnings there had been a labor imbalance in board composition, something rarely seen on any joint EAP committee. The Board's responsibilities included determining program policy, financial accountability, assessment of the overall effectiveness of the program, and appraisal of EAP staff. However, the Board was never given a formal budget for external counselling resulting in a perpetual underfunding of the EAP which became a critical issue during the University's organizational restructuring. The annual deficit had historically been dealt with by drawing upon a surplus that arose from the Program's initial start up being delayed by one year however, this fund had been exhausted and there was no longer any money available to provide for a service that continued to be offered.

Staff and faculty of the University and their family members also had varying levels of private extended health care benefits that were used to obtain additional counselling hours beyond what the EAP offered or instead of using the EAP. However, under the benefits plan counselling could only be obtained though the auspices of provincially registered psychologists, excluding other qualified and professionally registered professions. It also occasionally necessitated having an employee switch from a social worker or family counsellor, after the EAP-funded portion of their counselling allowance was exhausted, to a psychologist in order to allow for coverage through the extended benefits plan.

The internal EAP, itself, employed a system-based model, using a person-in-environment brief counselling protocol with referral to external sources for more complicated work. Table 1 provides a summary of program use between 1999 and 2004. A gradual decline in overall utilization can be observed that was reversed as the University entered its period of internal restructuring and reorganization. Likewise, clinical

TABLE 1. Program Utilization

Year	Employees	Clinical Intake	Consultations	Total	Clinical Utilization	Overall Utilization
1999	3617	188	196	384	5.2	10.6
2000	4465	234	190	424	5.2	9.5
2001	4465	243	124	376	5.4	8.2
2002	4465	281	154	435	6.2	9.7
2003	4465	292	168	460	6.5	10.3
2004	4465	350	207	557	7.8	12.4

use increased during this period of uncertainty which placed further stress upon an EAP already working at a maximum capacity which in turn was part of the reason for undertaking a broader review of the program, its structure and its future.

THE PROCESS

The review of the University of Saskatchewan Employee Assistance Program occurred between November 2005 and April 2006 and entailed a review of 29 documents including that which had triggered the organizational change process the *University of Saskatchewan Strategic Documents: Renewing the Dream A Framework for Action* (2002). Seven focus group meetings organized by stakeholder group consisting of 48 individuals were conducting along with nine individual interviews with representatives from throughout the university in December and ten in January who were unable to attend the scheduled focus groups. Thirteen individuals unable to attend either a focus group or an individual interview completed formal written responses to the focus group questions (Table 2). The seven focus groups held were for EAP staff, external service providers, the EAP Advisory Board, representatives of the major bargaining units, managers and supervisors, human resources staff, and members of the university administration.

All participants completed a consent form that discussed the scope of the review and how the data would be used. Participants also received a list of questions to be discussed prior to their focus group or key informant interview (Table 2). The focus group interview schedule was constructed by the Review Panel with feedback provided by the EAP committee and

TABLE 2. Focus Group Questions

1. What do you see as the role of the EAP program at the University of Saskatchewan?
2. Tell us a bit about how you see the EAP. Is it a stand alone service or is it integrated with other services such as occupational health and safety, occupational health, human resources? To what extent should it be?
3. In your opinion how should the EAP be situated within the University environment in terms of reporting relationship to best meet the needs of the three stakeholder groups: university administration, employees and the providers of service?
4. What are the greatest strengths of the current EAP program? What does it do well?
5. What do you see as the major weaknesses or shortfalls of the current program? What doesn't it do well?
6. Are there things the EAP should not be doing that it is currently involved in?
7. What innovative programs are in place, or could be developed to increase resilience and prevent the need for employee absence in the first place? Where does the EAP fit into this?
8. Of the services currently being offered what should be done by in-house staff versus outside contractors?
9. Who currently does the EAP serve in your opinion and whom should it serve?
10. How does the EAP determine success in your opinion?
11. How should success be determined?
12. Any final thoughts or comments that you'd like to discuss before we wrap up?

university administration on the initial draft. The final step in the program evaluation was a review of how other western Canadian universities provided EAPs services and administered their programs.

FINDINGS

The review was conducted in the midst of a major change process occurring at the University. As has been repeatedly shown even when adequate preparation and forewarning occurs organizational change processes are inherently stressful as employees adapt to changing and evolving environments and an uncertain employment landscape. The fact that the review of the EAP was occurring within and as a result of this process was one contributing factor to the high level of interest that was generated by this program evaluation and why most of the focus groups went over the allocated time without even addressing all of the pre-planned questions. There was much discussion in the focus groups regarding the potential integration of EAP services with human resources programs as in the minds of the majority of participants these two have inherently distinct functions. For many, integration implied some loss of confidentiality and the autonomy of the EAP. As such, the proposed integration of the two, as it was understood, was not supported by representatives of the various bargaining units. Individuals with administrative responsibilities were, on the contrary, generally supportive of the notion of integration, as they typically believed that the current EAP operated in isolation from other services that were intended to support and enhance individual and organizational well being such as disability management, health and physical wellness and return-to-work programs.

The evaluators noted that since the Employee Assistance Program had been implemented in 1989 little had changed in the operation of the program and in the supports the university provided to it and as a result several shortcomings had arisen. However, despite the limitations the reviewers were overwhelmed by the open and publicly stated support for and interest in the program as demonstrated during the site visits and through requests for individual meetings by those unable to attend along with unsolicited requests to forward written submissions. There was a genuine passion demonstrated for the EAP, what it had done, what it was doing and its potential for the future as the University of Saskatchewan entered its second one hundred years of service as an educational institution. While in many organizations little is known about EAP, at the University of Saskatchewan it was acknowledged as an integral program for employees and family members alike.

> *I cannot say enough about how much I owe (the EAP Director) and the EAP Program. I have managed to keep my family and my job, brought in large research grants over a very long period of time, have been nominated for teaching awards and contributed to my Department and to the University in numerous ways. I have no doubt that much of this would not have happened had I not gone to the U of S EAP.*
>
> *I would give EAP an A+++ based on the skill, kindness of the overworked but totally dedicated staff. (The director's) counselling skills are top notch.*
>
> *They provide options to the individual to make some choices that gives them hope to continue while they strive to achieve a different direction in life.*

The program evaluation indicated that the EAP had been providing the type of services it was created to do and that the majority of individuals who used the service saw it as a positive resource (Table 3). The EAP and its supporting external counselling services were most likely reducing institutional costs and the savings accrued likely exceed the cost of the program though no definitive return on investment value could be obtained through the parameters of the review. However, it is the unanimous opinion of the Review Panel that the EAP was significantly underfunded and under-resourced in its current configuration and was not in a position to meet the long term needs of the University. What was ground breaking in 1989 was no longer sufficient in 2006.

One result of program under funding over the years was that the director had had to take on a "gatekeeper" function. While this had helped to control costs, it was perceived by some university staff and external providers as a barrier to services, as a portion of employees would prefer to access alternative support services without going directly through the EAP. There were also a minority of University staff members, particularly faculty and administrators, who, for various reasons such as past history, dual relationships and concerns regarding anonymity were not comfortable with having to go through EAP to access counselling or support services. As well, despite qualifications, experience, training and education not all clients will connect with any one counsellor and research

TABLE 3. Client Satisfaction Results

Item	2003 n = 75 % satisfied/ very satisfied	2004 n = 89 % satisfied/ very satisfied
EAP responded promptly to my request for service	98.7	100
I was understood by the EAP counsellor	94.5	96.6
EAP staff demonstrated professional skill and demeanour	100	97.8
My EAP experience was treated confidentially	96.0	95.5
Follow-up by the EAP staff was useful	68.0	66.3
I would recommend the EAP to others	98.7	97.8
EAP was helpful in addressing my concerns	92.0	97.8
My coping ability improved through contact with the EAP	78.7	87.6
The issue was resolved to my satisfaction	60.0	57.3
If needed I would contact EAP again	92.0	97.7
Overall, I was satisfied with the EAP's services	94.7	97.7

has demonstrated that gender does make a difference in counselling (Dawson, 1996; Didham & Csiernik, 2006; Hodgins, el Guebaly, & Addington, 1997; Jarvis, 1992).

The original Program mandate had also indicated that education and training were to be core functions of the EAP. However, this initiative had been lost as demand for direct practice had increased over time. As well, the more complex, multi-dimensional, and/or workplace-related a problem scenario is, the more important it is for a variety of university services to be involved and coordinated in order to best assist the employee. The same applies to matters that are related to or affect employee performance especially in the areas of disability management, health and physical wellness and return-to-work issues, domains of human resources. Each of these programs emerged after the EAP was well established but little was done to connect the programs. As many clients involved with those programs often also became involved with the EAP ongoing communication and coordination between human resources and the Employee Assistance Program needed to be formalized addressed.

In examining the structure and accountability of other western Canadian university EAPs (Table 4) it was found that the vast majority had opted for an externally contracted model administered through the human resources division of the university. While six had either an exclusive joint labour-management EAP advisory committee or broader wellness board, four had no representative administrative structure to report through while one used an ad hoc system and one did not reply to the panel's inquiries.

RESULTS

This review provided an opportunity for the University of Saskatchewan to reconfigure an EAP that was conceptualized nearly two decades previously in a much different educational, organizational, societal and EAP context and to support the EAP in becoming an even better resource to meet the evolving needs of the University. Based upon the findings, current and common practices in the EAP field and the needs of the University a series of recommendations were made to the University administration and Associations through the EAP Advisory Committee to allow it to build upon its long history of assisting employees with personal issues through adopting an interdisciplinary multiple pathways approach. It was recommended that the EAP remain a neutral, independent, confidential program, working in a professional, cooperative,

TABLE 4. Western Canadian University EAP Structures

University	In-House/ Contracted	Accountable to Advisory or Management Board	Committee	Integration
University of Winnipeg	Contracted	Human Resources	Advisory	Prefer More
Brandon University	Contracted	Human Resources	None	None
University of Manitoba	Contracted Capped @6	Human Resources/ Benefits	Advisory	With Consent
University of Regina	no information received			
Athabasca Universtiy	Contracted	Human Resources	Wellness Advisory Committee	Rehab & HR Work-Life Consultants
University of Calgary	Contracted	AVP-HR	Wellness advisory Committee	Fully Integrated With Consent
University of Lethbridge	In-House	AVP-HR	None	Case-by-case
Simon Fraser University	Contracted 12 hours max	HR Manager	Advisory	None
University of British Colombia	Contracted with consent	AVP-HR	Advisory	case-by-case
University of Northern British Colombia (UNBC)	Contracted	Human Resources	None	None
University of Victoria	Contracted 10 hours max	Human Resources– Benefits Manager	None	Links with Health & Safety
Royal Roads University	Contracted	Human Resources when contract	ad hoc advisory tendered	integrated on a case-by-case basis

collaborative and appropriate manner with other campus-based professionals including human resources consultants, occupational health and safety personnel and the University's sexual harassment officer. The recommended components of the occupational assistance program were:

- an expanded on-site externally contracted program including voluntary referrals and recommended referrals from manager, supervisors and union personnel;

- an expanded direct access route to professional counselling utilizing the extended health benefits program that any employee can access independently from the EAP; and,
- the current services offered by the human resources department relating to disability management, health and physical wellness and return-to-work issues to remain under the management of human resources.

The Review Panel believed that the EAP should retain an on-site presence. This then led to the inevitable question: is it better to have the EAP staffed by employees of the organization to deliver the service, or is it more advantageous to out-source the program to a local provider? Out-sourcing the EAP has the potential to enhance the perception of neutrality and confidentiality and distance the EAP staff in appropriate manner from the internal dynamics of the University that continued to exist during the broader change process. However, internal staff have the opportunity to develop more casual relationships with various units and staff, thus allowing for greater informal contact and use of the Program. These types of contacts can lend themselves to a "value added" dynamic without additional costs (Csiernik, 1999). Ultimately the common practice of other universities in the geographic vicinity acted as the tipping variable and it was recommended that the University switch to an out-sourced model. However, it was also recommended that two additional dedicated counselling staff at the Masters level or above be added to the EAP staffing compliment, with at least one being female, and that the counselling team be physically housed on-site.

The program evaluators stated that three on-site counsellors would be better able to serve staff and families while still using a brief, systems-orientated, solution focused approach. However, time also needed to be devoted to developmental, educational, and administrative functions that were part of the initial program but that had been subsumed by counselling demands. As well, it was recommended that for clients with more complex problems and for those who preferred an external-based counsellor to staff located on the University campus that the external service provider component of the program should also be maintained. Research has found that capping services at low levels serves limited clinical purpose and has limited financial benefit as long as external counsellors are clearly aware of the focus of the EAP and they are monitored appropriately (Csiernik, 2002). Thus, along with and in support of counselling provided by the three on-site EAP staff, a maximum of $1000.00 per employee or dependent per year from $350.00 (with the amount to be monitored regularly and adjusted upward as required) was recommended to be allocated for those referred externally by EAP staff. The $1000.00 annual limit was also recommended for those who preferred to use the extended benefits program and find their own counsellor without contacting the EAP. As well, it was further recommended that the extended benefits plan should be amended to allow for counselling by any counsellor at the Masters Level or higher of any professionally recognized and regulated profession.

In examining the administrative aspects of the program, it was recommended that the function of the EAP Committee should shift from being a management board to that of an advisory committee. Supervision of staff should become the responsibility of the out-sourced provider rather than of university volunteers while the budget should become the responsibility of the human resources department to allow for adequate financing of the expanded program. It was also recommended that he EAP Advisory Committee should consist of an equal number of labor and management representatives, which would necessitate a change to the various collective agreements, which in itself is a detailed and intricate process. The Review Panel also stated that the committee should be led by two co-chairs, one representing management, the other labor. The EAP Advisory Committee should also become accountable to the Associate Vice President of Human Resources for administrative and financial purposes rather than the Vice President of Finance and Administration as has become common practice among university EAPs throughout western Canada.

Once the renewed EAP was in place a more systematic formalized orientation program and ongoing promotion and awareness campaign was recommended to be developed for all staff and family members including developing an easily recognizable and distinct EAP "brand" and design to develop a unique identity for this highly valued University resource. This process should be led by the campus-based EAP staff providing the opportunity to create a profile within the University community. To further enhance the well being of the workplace it was also recommended that EAP staff undertake or sponsor a regular series of proactive and preventative workshops/seminars/brown bag lunches on issues pertinent to the well being of the workplace and the organization, again using the to be designed EAP "brand." Finally, as part of the restructuring all existing policies and procedures needed to be collected into one comprehensive policy document and updated based upon the renewed University of Saskatchewan Employee Assistance Program.

CONCLUSION

Few EAPs totally disappear once they have been initiated. However, they can go on their helpful though merry ways with evaluation limited to an annual report that typically indicates how many people were seen and how satisfied they were. This in and of itself is not a bad thing however it does not address the fact that like organizations, EAPs are not static entities and that they too need to change, evolve and adapt. Most organizations look vastly different in 2006 than they did in 1989–can the same be said of EAPs established to support both employees and organizations? Have the changes that have occurred in typical EAPs over the course of the past two decades been reflexive, a response to marketing, or part of a more detailed, systematic process, not necessarily as extensive as that conducted in this case study by the University of Saskatchewan, but still more than a two hour brain storming session attended by a half dozen vested stakeholders? As well, without joint committees to guide and direct EAPs who is left to read and respond to even the humble annual report, the most basic element in EAP evaluation? For as is seen in this article, in western Canada, not even all institutions founded upon creating and sharing knowledge in an environment of academic freedom had an internal place to share this knowledge about the wellness of their own organizations.

The process of EAP renewal that occurred and that is occurring at the University of Saskatchewan was hardly painless. While conversations and debates remained professional there were many disagreements, needed cooling off periods, multiple and repeated discussions of the same theme and yet it was always with the goal of enhancing what was a sound idea and what was a fundamentally good program. The EAP had champions in all sectors of the University and existing staff were supported by many quarters but this does not take away the reality that transition and change have become the norm of the working world and are the very context for much of the counselling done by EAPs. However, in this case study it was the EAP itself that was the focus of this transitional process and change rather than the resource to facilitate it.

What is not yet known, as the new program is only now being implemented, is the impact that these changes will have upon the University as a whole. Will these changes in fact improve the provision of assistance or perhaps detract from what had been a well established program or even have no discernable impact at all, and what would that say about the process? As the University of Saskatchewan enters its second century of providing post-secondary education and the EAP enters its second decade of providing support it can only be hoped that the need for change, evolution and adaptation will become integrated into both and become the norm for both and that it will be a functional change and not one that occurs simply because.

REFERENCES

Csiernik, R. (1999). Internal versus external Employee Assistance Programs: What the Canadian data adds to the debate. *Employee Assistance Quarterly, 15*(2), 1-12.

Csiernik, R. (2002). An overview of Employee and Family Assistance Programming in Canada. *Employee Assistance Quarterly, 18*(1), 17-34.

Dawson, D.A. (1996). Gender differences in the probability of alcohol treatment. *Journal of Substance Abuse, 8*(2), 211-225.

Didham, S. & Csiernik, R. (2006). Does sex matter? Gender differences in addiction counselling. *Addiction Professional, 4*(2), 44-46.

Hodgins, D.C., El-Guebaly, N., & Addington, J. (1997). Treatment of substance abusers: single or mixed gender programs? *Addiction, 92*(7), 805-812.

Jarvis, T.J. (1992). Implications of gender for alcohol treatment research: a quantitative and qualitative review. *British Journal of Addiction, 87*(9), 1249-1261.

University of Saskatachewan (1993). *University of Saskatchewan mission statement.* Retrieved June 26, 2006, from http://www.usask.ca/uofs/mission.html.

University of Saskatcewan (2002). *University of Saskatchewan strategic documents: Renewing the dream a framework for action.* Saskatoon.

University of Saskatchewan (2003). *A new vision for human resources at the University of Saskatchewan: Transforming human resources into a strategic asset-human resources division multi-year plan 2003-2007.* Saskatoon.

doi:10.1300/J490v22n03_04

Enhancing Faculty Access: A Cultural Challenge for EAPs in Academe

John B. Franz

SUMMARY. Employee Assistance Programs (EAPs) in university settings have historically experienced significantly lower rates of usage by faculty than by staff. This fact has prompted interest in developing strategies that will identify and reduce barriers to access and increase the use of EAP services by academics. Using both participant observation and a review of the literature on faculty culture, five characteristics of academic life are identified that help explain faculty resistance to EAP services. Strategies designed to successfully enhance participation will incorporate these factors in their design. Several examples are offered and suggestions for future research are identified. doi:10.1300/J490v22n03_05 *[Article copies available for a fee from The Haworth Document Delivery Service: 1-800-HAWORTH. E-mail address: <docdelivery@haworthpress.com> Website: <http://www.HaworthPress.com> © 2006/2007 by The Haworth Press, Inc. All rights reserved.]*

KEYWORDS. EAP, academia, academic culture, faculty, higher education

[Haworth co-indexing entry note]: "Enhancing Faculty Access: A Cultural Challenge for EAPs in Academe." Franz, John B. Co-published simultaneously in *Journal of Workplace Behavioral Health* (The Haworth Press, Inc.) Vol. 22, No. 2/3, 2006/2007, pp. 57-73; and: *Employee Assistance Programs in Higher Education* (ed: R. Paul Maiden and Sally B. Philips) The Haworth Press, 2006/2007, pp. 57-73. Single or multiple copies of this article are available for a fee from The Haworth Document Delivery Service [1-800-HAWORTH, 9:00 a.m. - 5:00 p.m. (EST). E-mail address: docdelivery@haworthpress.com].

Available online at http://jwbh.haworthpress.com

doi:10.1300/J490v22n03_05

INTRODUCTION

Faculty Usage of EAP Services

The underutilization of employee assistance program (EAP) services by faculty has been a topic of interest virtually since the inception of EAPs in academe over thirty years ago (Roman, 1980, Thoreson & Hosokawa, 1984). While little substantive research has examined this phenomenon in depth, over the years this fact has been consistently observed and occasionally documented by those in academe: EAPs in higher education experience much higher utilization by staff than by faculty.

Research by Mermis (1989) of some fifty EAP higher education programs indicated that faculty typically comprised less than 20% of the universities' EAP clients, while staff constituted up to 89% of his sample's clientele. Sullivan and Poverny's (1992) study of staff/faculty utilization in a major California university EAP showed a 4:1 ratio of staff to faculty. Their research also found junior faculty were more likely to use EAP services than their senior counterparts. In the author's twenty (20) years of EAP service in a regional university in the West, annual program statistics at his institution reflected a similar pattern. Consistently, faculty EAP program usage ranged from 13% to 24% of the approximately 350 cases serviced each year over two decades. Note, in many universities (including the author's) faculty comprise a smaller proportion of the total employee population than do staff so the EAP usage figures cited do not reveal the proportion of the institutions' overall faculty population who utilize the program's services.

Gross et al. (1996) national survey of 115 university EAPs revealed remarkably similar proportions. Faculty comprised from 13% to 24% of the clients in the institutions surveyed. They observed that "faculty, more than any other group, do not use the EAP as much as their representation in the overall workforce suggests they should." This national survey echoed faculty usage statistics presented in the above reports. It did not, however, provide a rationale for the results obtained.

A variety of explanations for patterns of low faculty EAP usage are offered in the few studies addressing this topic. Early speculation centered on the flexible nature of the university workplace, a type of "professional bureaucracy" stressing the value of independence and autonomy (Roman, 1980; Mintzberg, 1979). Sullivan and Poverny (1992) cited several studies which identified organizational conditions unique to higher education where "structured disadvantage" contributes to uneven

EAP use patterns. Examples included "flexible scheduling, a flattened organizational hierarchy, creativity, individualism and collegial relationships." Other studies associated the influence of collegiality with a preference for peer-referrals over more traditional supervisory EAP referrals (Gottlieb, 1984; Grosch et al., 1996).

There are a number of plausible but untested explanations that may be proposed to account for low faculty EAP participation. Included are resistance due to lack of confidence in the credentials of the employee assistance (EA) counselor, gender issues (male dominated workforce less likely to participate in counseling), age cohort factors (older persons less open to utilize one-on-one counseling/consultation), peer pressure, educational arrogance (e.g., 'PhDs shouldn't have to seek help'), confidentiality/privacy concerns, greater access to resources (financial and informational) by faculty and cultural/racial biases.

Faculty EAP usage, though proportionately smaller, is never-the-less significant in university contexts. Grosch and colleagues (1996) support Mintzberg's observation that "faculty are already the dominant or driving force on most campuses." They contend their research demonstrates "*perceived EAP effectiveness* [is] positively associated with faculty participation in the EAP" (emphasis added).

The central role faculty play in the academy has provided strong motivation for EA professionals to consider how best to meet faculty needs and encourage their participation and support of campus programs. Workshops and presentations with titles like "Reaching the reluctant faculty member" (John Hyatt, IAEAPE Annual Conference, San Francisco, November 16, 2004) have been a frequent topic at annual conferences of the International Association of Employee Assistance Professionals in Education (IAEAPE). Special outreach strategies to faculty have been proposed (Stoer-Scaggs, 1990). University services have changed their program names from Employee Assistance to Faculty and Staff Assistance in order to attract faculty (S. Philips, personal communication, September 28, 2004). Some institutions of higher education (e.g., University of Minnesota, and University of Texas, MD Anderson Hospital) have created separate faculty-exclusive EAP programs, policies and services to better serve this group.

Two lingering questions, however, remain largely unanswered. What factors associated with academic life inhibit faculty from participating in employee assistance services? What can EA professionals do to more effectively overcome resistance and serve the needs of academics on their campus? It is to the examination of these questions that our discussion now turns.

EXPLORING THE INFLUENCE OF FACULTY CULTURE

In the spirit of observational research, by adopting an "ethnographic approach" (Agar, 1996; Ganzuk, 2003) the author will share his reflections on faculty culture and discuss the concomitant implications for improving services to and increasing participation of academics in campus EAPs. Ethnography is a phenomenological mode of inquiry for producing knowledge and for studying organizational culture (O'Neill, 1998). According to John Van Maanen (1996), "When used as a method, ethnography typically refers to fieldwork (alternatively, participant-observation) conducted by a single investigator who 'lives with and lives like' those who are studied."

After twenty years as a full-time Director of a university EAP program in a regional university in the West, I (the author) exercised previously granted "retreat rights," leaving my management position on the administrative side to assume a new assignment as a full-time tenured professor in an academic department on campus. Though I had taught individual courses in an adjunct role each semester for most of my years at the university, the move into the faculty ranks generated fresh insights into the academic world and an inside view of the academy to which I simply had not previously had access. Initially, it also provoked what might be characterized as a form of 'culture shock.'

Before offering some personal reflections on the nature of faculty life and its relevance to Employee Assistance services, a cautionary note should be sounded. In addition to the obvious concern with observer subjectivity, what about the *object* of the observations? To what extent is it legitimate to generalize about faculty culture? Silver (2003) addresses the question even more pointedly in an article titled, "Does a university have a culture?" Typical of comments from his literature review are those of Barnett (cited in Silver, 2003):

"We cannot assume that the manifold activities of the 'multiversity' have anything in common. It follows that the notion that there could be a single binding characteristic that all constituent parts of the university share, that there could be an essence, has to be suspect."

Silver concludes, "Asserting that there is a 'dominant culture' simply bypasses the issues of conflict and lack of coherence . . . Universities do not now have an organizational culture" (2003). Clark (1985) likewise, warns "whoever generalizes about 'the faculty' or 'the professoriate' does so on thin ice."

Silver (2003) and Clark's (1985) conclusions appropriately caution regarding the problems inherent in uncritical generalizing about an endeavor as diverse and complex as academic life. They are challenged, however, by the efforts of a host of other scholars, who have drawn a different set of conclusions about the viability of describing faculty life in cultural terms (e.g., Ayers, 2004; Bila & Miller, 1997; Bohen & Schuster, 1986; Kuh & Whitt, 1988; O'Meara, 2004; Srikanthan & Dalrymple, 2002; Tierney, 1988). Adopting this contrasting heuristic perspective, one may cautiously examine the behavior of academic professionals. Tierney and Rhoads (as cited in Hardesty, 1995) represent this point of view. "While faculty may be quite diverse across institutional type and discipline, they nonetheless perform many similar tasks, share common values and beliefs, and identify with one another as colleagues." It is from this vantage point reflections which follow are offered.

OBSERVATIONS OF FACULTY CULTURE

Observation #1: The Primary Professional Commitment of Faculty Is to Their Particular Discipline

Relationships within academic departments, however, are more fragmented or diverse than unified and cohesive.

This is a perspective that is well supported in the literature (see Barnett, 1990, 2000; Barton & Rowland, 2003; Becher & Trowler, 2001; Dill, 1982). Sanford (1971) identified the respecting of specialty bounds as one of the 'rules' of faculty culture. Silver (2003) notes "the strength of commitment to the discipline [is] the cornerstone of personal interest, career and professional activity and identity" in the academy.

When I moved into a faculty role, I anticipated joining a relatively cohesive group of professionals, engaging in common endeavor stimulated by civil discourse, and sharing not only adjacent space but an acknowledged sense of purpose and community. What I encountered instead, were clusters of discipline-bounded professionals, largely preoccupied with their particular course assignments and research interests. Interpersonal relationships within my department and others nearby were more often marked by internal cliques and periodic flare-ups than defined by warm and cohesive friendships.

Faculty members from nearby academic departments did not often mix with those from my discipline. The reverse was also true. Professors rarely interacted outside of their disciplines unless they met on campus committees. Within my department and in neighboring faculty units there appeared more often to be pairings and subgroups based on shared philosophy or points of view than broader collegial affiliations.

As a former manager accustomed to standard business hours, I was initially puzzled at how few of my faculty colleagues were to be found in their offices during the course of the day. When queried, fellow academics indicated that they only kept required on-campus office hours for advising and attending certain meetings; they favored working at home to avoid distractions and to increase productivity. This practice, however attractive and helpful to goal-minded professors, clearly reduced opportunities for interaction and limited the exchange of informal communication.

Alexander Austin's comments (quoted in Silver, 2003) summarize my initial impressions:

". . . the 'community' of scholars remains more of an ideal than a reality. We have the scholars, to be sure, but we lack the community. One might more aptly characterize the modern university as a 'collection' rather than a community of scholars."

One of the more substantial points of divergence in academic departments has to do with differences in rank and experience. I observed that there was a well-acknowledged status hierarchy in my department. Junior faculty (untenured) carried significantly higher work loads than most of their senior (tenured) counterparts, especially in terms of committee work. Bila & Miller (1997) explored the differences between junior and senior faculty. They found junior faculty to be markedly more optimistic and less cynical and they were responsible for more of the perceived workload in on-campus activities than their senior counterparts. Those in the senior ranks, on the other hand, enjoyed greater degrees of power and influence but tended to be more skeptical and negative, especially toward administrators.

In sum, my observations suggest that it is a mistake to assume that broad personal or professional interests and consensus exists in the professorate. EAP outreach strategies that make this assumption and fail to account for differences in the experience, rank and department-based interests of academics are unlikely to be productive.

Observation #2: Autonomy, A Core Faculty Value, Is Both the Best Friend and Worst Enemy of Competence and Success in Academic Careers

Hardesty (1995) observes that "One of the most prevalent canons of faculty culture is that the faculty member has complete professional autonomy." Ayers (2004) uses the phrase "profoundly autonomous" to describe life in the academy. He suggests that "our fragmented institutions are unified mainly by people's common willingness to allow others to pursue their own, often incomprehensible expertise."

One of the most attractive features of entering academic life as a professor was the freedom to determine much of my daily schedule and tasks. My classes and office hours are scheduled events (that I have freedom to cancel with little justification), but how I choose to spend the rest of my time is up to me. I discovered later starts and earlier exits from the office to be a pleasant change. As noted above, the presence on campus of most faculty I observed was largely limited to time spent in class or in assigned responsibilities, such as formal meetings and the advising of students.

Another evidence of autonomy in academe is the freedom faculty members enjoy to teach classes as they wish, largely without any oversight and with minimum feedback. O'Meara's (2004) research found that faculty resisted evaluation, especially peer review. Their subjects insisted that it was inappropriate, non-collegial and just plain difficult to do, especially for tenured (senior) professors. Hardesty's (1995) review of literature on evaluation of teaching found that most faculty members do not even discuss their teaching with colleagues.

In my experience, faculty with strong work values and initiative transform the freedom from close scrutiny into increased opportunities for creativity. This autonomy is translated into impressive investments of time and energy spent in infusing technology and introducing innovative learning strategies. Conversely, and sadly, however, the lack of accountability may also lead to poor instruction and inappropriate work behavior, such as canceling classes on a whim, skipping meetings and committees, and neglecting advising and mentoring obligations. Unless students complain (they are reluctant to do so) this behavior rarely comes to the attention of department or university officials. Autonomy may also lead to grade inflation (Johnson, 2003) and the "justification of unusual personal liberties" (Clark cited in Hardesty, 1995). My observations of faculty behavior would concur with the full range of the above comments.

What is most striking to me about the issue of autonomy, however, is the degree to which it appears to define the mind-set of fellow academicians. Any suggestions by campus administration of 'mandatory' training or 'required attendance' (e.g., for sexual harassment workshops) are almost sure to evoke strong resistance and testing by faculty. Administrative directives or efforts to force change, whether major or incidental, are predictably and consistently perceived negatively through this lens.

EAP strategies to reach faculty that fail to respect their autonomy are unlikely to be met with success and may actually result in undermining institutional support for the service itself.

Observation #3: One of the Prevalent Themes in Faculty Life Is the Persistent Perception of a Lack of Time

Hardesty (1995) cites a variety of different studies that highlight the open-endedness of work in academic life. "All competent faculty members live with the sense that they are dealing with infinity–that they can never fully catch up" (Bowen & Schuster, cited in Hardesty). This is especially true for new faculty and for those with a high achievement orientation. Meetings with students, committee work, professional conferences, research, writing, mentoring, attending academically related social events, conducting peer evaluations, reading and preparing class presentations, correcting papers–the list of duties seems endless. Many of these activities are not obvious to those outside of the academy. Because of the autonomy that accompanies their role, faculty themselves have the ability to determine how they wish to allocate their time. There is some evidence (Harry & Goldner, cited in Hardesty, 1995) that any extra time academics devote to research comes not from teaching but from their leisure and family activities.

I found it quite a paradox that the greater freedom and autonomy I embraced in my change of assignment from EAP Director to professor were followed so quickly by the feeling of being behind in my duties. Informal conversations with my academic colleagues were almost inevitably marked by some sort of statement of how much they had to do or how busy they were. I found myself quickly adopting this habit in my responses as well.

A partial explanation for the lack of time faculty decry may be found in the surprising extent to which bureaucratic demands from university administration impinge upon one's schedule. The rise of "managerialism" with its more formalized structures and rationalized processes has invaded the academy (Barton & Rowland, 2003). Srikanthan & Dalrymple (2002) indicate that this trend is increasingly being met by a conservative counter-reaction from faculty that they term "cloisterism." I certainly found myself resisting requests for activity reports, updated vita and website information, travel proposals and post-travel reports, surveys, book orders, mission statement revisions, peer reviews of teaching, and student reference letters to name a few of the new bureaucratic requests I had to address. None of these activities helped me to prepare for my classes or write a journal article.

Successful outreach strategies must take into account the nearly universal sense that faculty have of being behind in their work. A case must be made for why EAP sponsored services or activities are of vital concern and need to be made a priority. If conducting research typically 'trumps' leisure and home life activity, how will EAP service trump research?

Observation #4: Individually, Faculty Present as Personable, Decisive and Focused; Collectively, Posturing, Delays, Compromise, and Resistance to Change Characterize Their Group Dynamics

Hardesty (1995) observes that "faculty members have become well known for their resistance to change." He notes that they tend to be conservative in their approach to the "academic process" preferring to bypass the details and demands of university procedures and operations whenever possible. Academics resent instructional innovations that will require adaptation of well-established patterns. For example, text and curriculum changes typically require faculty to alter familiar lecture notes, to redo power points, to research new illustrations and to update data. One can expect such changes to be viewed skeptically and initially to meet with resistance (Bergquist, 1992). Concerns about time pressure noted earlier factor into this pattern, but faculty resistance is probably more philosophical and value-based (autonomy) than practical.

The historic value of collegiality in academe prompts a strong expectation of faculty *governance by consensus*. Combining their perceptions of time pressure, skepticism toward change and a penchant for intellectualizing, it is perhaps not surprising that decision-making in academic departments is ponderous at best. Cohen and March (1974) popularized the metaphor of an 'organized anarchy' to describe the functioning of institutional subunits. As Silver (2003) observed: "The contemporary university may be conceived as a 'culture of tolerance of diversity,' a 'culture of extreme diversity' or a 'culture of fragmentation in tension' . . ." However they may be appraised, what transpires in department meetings is more about the people than the agenda.

One of the most challenging experiences I encountered upon joining an academic department was that of attending its formal meetings. These events were billed as opportunities for information sharing, cordial debate around decision-making and the development of community. Informally, they allowed for recognition of rank and experience, and for socializing junior faculty into the values and mores of the unit. Occasionally, faculty meetings became a place to vent and confront. In my department, most of the exchanges were civil, though largely non-conclusive. In other departments, I was told, exchanges sometimes became demeaning and caustic.

I did not experience, however, faculty meetings as I had imagined them to be: settings where common concerns were rationally processed and consensus regularly achieved. I found them to be markedly non-productive time-consuming events, dominated by a few senior spokespersons, more often demonstrating the diversity of opinions that were present than unity of purpose. Bila & Miller (1997) observed that department power tends to be concentrated in cynical, radical-sounding, senior faculty who distrust administration and consider themselves as innovative and creative survivors. Their descriptions might have come from observing some of our meetings. The trust, enthusiasm, appreciation for academe, and overwhelmed persona the researchers attributed to junior faculty were also evident in our department gatherings.

Whenever EAP strategies for connecting with faculty propose department-wide participation, they need to factor in the challenges noted above. Entrenched resistance to change, difficulty in achieving consensus, and the politics of rank and power in academic departments provide impressive obstacles not typically encountered by EA programs when presenting team-building experiences and workshops to staff groups.

Observation #5: The Drive for Recognition Is the Single Most Significant Motivator of Faculty in the Academy

According to Ayres (2004) "Reputation is the only measurable index of success (in the academy) . . . awards, prizes and titles often replace money as indexes of success; other than the military, this is the only American institution in which this is so." Hermanowicz (2005) asserts, "The institutionalized drive for recognition ultimately exists as the common denominator among all (academic) fields." The criteria for faculty success and failure in academe is generally defined and made meaningful by their peers–in their department, institution and professional discipline (Hermanowicz 2005; Silver, 2003). This icon of faculty culture provides one of the most powerful means of understanding the behavior of academics, both in what they choose and in what they avoid.

I observed that tenure-track faculty in my department tended to avoid committees, tasks and activities that carried little potential for enhancing their recognition or status. This applied to maintenance activities like a committee to plan graduation activities, or a task force to reword syllabus language or a subgroup to order library materials. It also applied to volunteer activities such as presenting a workshop for staff, sponsoring a student club or joining a holiday food drive. I suspect it explains why so few faculty attended our EAP-sponsored campus work/life programs.

On the other hand, when invitations were extended to lead, present or participate in high profile events, (e.g., a conference, symposium or community lecture series) I witnessed a very different response by my colleagues. The need for documentation in the tenure process, the pressures of time and responsibilities discussed earlier, and the inherent nature of establishing expertise, all help explain the preference for recognition by junior faculty. The pattern continues to persist, however, in tenured, senior faculty as well.

The drive for recognition and affirmation by peers also has a down side. Faculty learn early-on (e.g., from dissertation committees) that the opinions of professional peers are important and carry potential career-impacting consequences. I observed cautiousness in my faculty colleagues regarding casual sharing of personal information with their peers. I suspect the concern is that somehow this information might cloud the perceptions and opinions of others and thereby limit future professional opportunities. In a report of resistance to peer feedback in post-tenure review, O'Meara (2004) quotes a late-career faculty member's concern: ". . . this kind of thing is better for therapy–not the business of the university. The university has no right to tread into things that belong in a psychiatrist's office."

The above discussion and quote suggests that faculty is very cautious about the selection of those with whom they consult regarding problems or weaknesses, be they personal or professional. Their concern is heightened if the person or service consulted is campus-based, as most university EAPs are, for instance. Outreach strategies that do not address this issue, and that fail to take into account faculty recognition needs, are unlikely to be successful.

IMPLICATIONS FOR ENHANCING FACULTY EAP USAGE

The above observations of faculty culture have identified several factors that may help to explain the limited participation of faculty in campus EAP programs. The remaining discussion will consider implications for reaching academics more effectively. Based on the factors discussed in this paper, campus EAPs may want to consider designing or expanding their services in some of the following ways:

Overcoming Stigma

It is important to educate faculty regarding steps taken by the campus EAP to protect their privacy and confidentiality and to reduce the stigma faculty associate with EA consultations. This would be a good issue to submit to "evidence-based" change. Drawing from the experience of those programs that have uniquely served a faculty constituency, it would be useful to probe the significance of potential barriers to faculty participation such as EA counselor credentials (MA/MSW vs. Ph.D.), EA office location, and the perceived value of personal counseling/consultation. Psycho-educational presentations that touch on real professional needs of faculty (e.g., time management, overcoming writer's block, creative stress-management, managing classroom conflict) would be good empirical tests to the thesis of this paper, that meaningfully entering the culture will bridge the gap in EAP access.

Education regarding the benefits and advantages of EAP consultation is also useful information for skeptical academics. Since faculty value choice and autonomy, explaining how psychotherapy works, identifying community resources, and indicating how to choose a counselor or service might be examples of good additions to an EAP website that can be privately perused.

Studies noted earlier indicated a faculty preference for peer referrals. Thought might thus be given to developing or expanding such a referral system. Peer referrals to EAPs have been successful prompts for skeptical constituents in various research studies (Bacharach, Bamberger & McKinney, 2000; Bamberger & Sonnenstuhl, 1995; Bennett & Lehman, 2001). Hills and Johnson's (1989) REACH program, while developed in a community college setting, demonstrates the "power of peers in employee assistance" and suggests this as a valuable strategy to explore in other higher education settings.

Recognizing Differences

Faculty differ in their attitudes and needs, depending upon where they are in their respective careers. This fact presents another excellent opportunity for EAP programs to survey the concerns of this diverse component of their campus workforce. Younger faculty are more receptive to using EAP services. Their common needs for assistance in balancing work and family pressures may open opportunities for peer group support. Support groups may be especially attractive for junior faculty who are relatively isolated in their departments by gender or ethnic differences. Examples of seminar topics that may help build relationships with junior faculty: balancing work and family life, successful networking, finding a mentor, grant writing, authoring and getting published (book). Senior faculty may respond to topics such as addressing financial investments, eldercare, retirement planning, and leadership opportunities to name a few common late-career issues. These are interests in need of confirmation for the culturally sensitive EAP Director.

In view of the negative attitudes many senior faculty hold toward university administration, referenced earlier, EA professionals would be wise to use care in identifying too closely with campus leaders if they wish to reach this group. Recasting educational offerings as 'seminars' rather than 'workshops' may also appeal to the status needs of some faculty.

Servicing Academic Departments

Since the primary professional commitments of faculty are to their department or discipline, EAP outreach strategies should include initiating contact with individual academic units. This proposed innovation is largely unexplored. Focus groups with department chairs would be both a good way to probe potential interest in some sort of EA service to individual departments. It may also provide a means of developing a cultural vocabulary for future outreach efforts designed to target academic groups. By responding to identified unit needs such team building, conflict management, and strategic planning, for example, campus based EA professionals may soften skeptical attitudes toward the value of their services and open doors for future individual faculty contact. Such efforts may also contribute to the building of a needed sense of community in academic units referenced earlier. Busy and preoccupied faculty would appear far less likely to respond to a campus-wide program or activity than to an event tailored specifically to their own department. This is an assertion in need of empirical and practical examination.

Enhancing Reputations

EAP programs can tap into the self interest of faculty by finding ways to highlight their expertise and enhance their reputation in the campus community. Creating practical seminars or informational forums in which invited faculty can share their research or expertise with staff or peers is one way to build reputations and add value in the eyes of faculty. Other strategies to test this approach to relationship building include posting faculty produced health or wellness research on the EAP website, and sending personal email or notes to acknowledge individual faculty achievements announced to the campus. Faculty have a wealth of knowledge that may not be readily accessed by their own institutions. Another vehicle for enhancing faculty reputations may be for perceptive EA professionals to bring organizational needs and challenges (e.g., in marketing academic programs, in human resource training, in landscape design, in nutrition/food services, in program evaluation) to the attention of faculty who are experts in those areas, or who have conducted research that is relevant to such specific campus needs. The use of skillful internal networking by a campus EA professional may thus generate an additional source of benefit for both parties. This is an untested strategy for enhancing faculty EAP usage.

SUGGESTIONS FOR FUTURE RESEARCH

There are several potential lines of inquiry suggested by this paper. First, the literature on EAPs in higher education is sparse. The few studies that exist are dated and limited in scope. There is a need for more accurate and current descriptive information on EAPs in academe. More specifically, research is needed on the experience of various program models–internal and contractual–in serving faculty as well as staff.

Second, each of the five observations made in this paper contain assertions that merit empirical testing in relation to EAP usage by faculty. For example, does faculty usage increase when EAPs employ outreach strategies that take into account differences in experience, rank and department affiliation? Does it make a difference to take extra measures to protect and ensure confidentiality for faculty who may wish to consult their EAP but fear their autonomy may be compromised? Is perceived time pressure related to lower EAP usage by academics? Can EAPs offer meaningful services to academic departments, and if so, will that prompt individual faculty to use the services in greater numbers? Will recognition of faculty along with other relationship–building efforts narrow the gap and increase the frequency of faculty access to EAP services?

Finally, the discussion of strategies stimulated by our review of faculty culture offer several additional opportunities for researchers. Research is needed to confirm the primary barriers to EAP usage by faculty. The effectiveness of stigma-reducing efforts including attention to EA professional credentials, office location, service education/information and even the employing of peer referral strategies should be empirically assessed. Similarly, the viability of the proposal to target the needs of faculty at different stages in their careers and to tailor EA services to academic departments, needs to be explored. Will indirect relationship-building strategies such as those noted above increase interest and decrease resistance by faculty to EAP services? In sum, research is needed to examine the basic premise of this paper: if EA professionals employ strategies informed by research on faculty culture, will it result in increased program usage by the academic members of the community?

CONCLUSION

Research has shown that faculty under-utilize university based EAP services. The reasons for this fact may well be related to unique elements of faculty culture. This paper has explored the research on faculty culture and, together with the author's reflections as a participant-observer, has attempted to identify several factors that may help explain why faculty do not make better use of their campus EAP. Finally, some suggestions and implications for creating better utilization of these valuable services have been proposed and suggestions for future research have been identified.

REFERENCES

Agar, M. (1996). *The professional stranger: An informal introduction to ethnography.* San Diego, CA: *Academic* Press.

Bacharach, S. B., Bamberger, P. & McKinney, V. (2000, December). Boundary management tactics and logics of action: The case of peer-support providers. *Administrative Science Quarterly, 45*(4), 704-736.

Bamberger, P. & Sonnenstuhl, W. J. (1995). Peer referral networks and utilization of a union-based EAP. *Journal of Drug Issues, 25*(2), 291-312.

Barnett, R. (1990). *The idea of higher education.* Buckingham, England: Open University Press.

Barnett, R. (2000). *Realizing the university in an age of supercomplexity.* Buckingham: Open University Press.

Barton, L. & Rowland, S. (2003). An interview with Geoff Whitty & Michael Worton. *Teaching in Higher Education, 8*(4), 563-578.

Becher, T. & Trowler, P. (2001). *Academic tribes and territories: Intellectual enquiry and the cultures of discipline* (2nd ed.). Stony Stratford, England: Open University Press.

Bennett, J. B. & Lehman, W. (2001, July). Workplace substance abuse prevention and help seeking: Comparing team-oriented and informational training. *Journal of Occupational Health Psychology, 6*(3), 243-254.

Bergquist, W. H. (1992). *The four cultures of the academy: Insights and strategies for improving leadership in collegiate organizations.* San Francisco: Jossey-Bass.

Bila, T. A. & Miller, M. T. (1997, January). *College faculty cultures: Dominance in the academy.* Report of a paper presented at the Annual Conference of the Popular Culture Association (Honolulu, HI).

Bowen, H. R. & Schuster, J. H. (1986). *American professors: A national resource imperiled.* New York: Oxford University Press.

Clark, B. R. (1985). Listening to the professoriate. *Change, 17*(5), 36-43.

Cohen, M. D. & March, J. G. (1974). *Leadership and ambiguity: The American college president.* New York: McGraw-Hill.

Dill, D. D. (1982). The management of academic culture: Notes on the management of meaning and social integration. *Higher Education, 11*, 303-320.

Genzuk, M. (2003, Fall). *A synthesis of ethnographic research.* Occasional Papers Series. Center for Multilingual, Multicultural Research (Eds.). Rossier School of Education, University of Southern California, Los Angeles.

Gottlieb, B. H. (1984). The informal system of employee assistance on campus. In R. W. Thoreson & E. P. Hosokawa (Eds.), *Employee assistance programs in higher education.* Springfield, IL: Charles C. Thomas.

Gross, J. W., Duffy, K. G., & Hessink, T. K. (1996). Employee assistance programs in higher education: Factors associated with program usage and effectiveness. *Employee Assistance Quarterly, 11*(4), 43-57.

Hardesty, L. (1995). Faculty culture and bibliographic instruction: An exploratory analysis. *Library Trends, 44*(2), 339-368.

Hermanowicz, J. C. (2005, January-February). Classifying universities and their departments: A social world perspective. *Journal of Higher Education, 76*(1), 26-56.

Hill, M. D., Johnson, P., Michalenko, C., Docherty, O., et al. (1989, January). The power of peers in employee assistance: A unique program for a community college. *The Journal of Canadian Counselling, 23*(1), 67-74.

Johnson, V. (2003). *Grade inflation: A crisis in higher education.* New York: Springer-Verlag New York, Inc.

Kuh, G. D., & Whitt, E. J. (1988). *The invisible tapestry: Culture in American colleges and universities.* ASHE-ERIC Higher Education Report, No. 1. Washington, DC: Association for the Study of Higher Education.

Mermis, W. L. (1990, February). The college and university EAP network. *EAPA Exchange,* 34-35.

Mintzberg, H. (1979). *The structuring of organizations.* Englewood Cliffs, NH: Prentice Hall.

O'Meara, K. A. (2004, March-April). Beliefs about post-tenure review: The influence of autonomy, collegiality, career stage, and institutional context. *Journal of Higher Education, 75*(2), 178-203.

O'Neill, B. J. (1998, December). Institutional ethnography: Studying institutions from the margins. *Journal of Sociology and Social Welfare, 25*(4), 127-144.

Roman, P. M. (1980). Employee alcoholism and assistance programs: Adapting an innovation for college and university faculty. *Journal of Higher Education, 51*, 135-149.

Sanford, N. (1971). Academic culture and the teacher's development. *Soundings, 54*(4), 357-371.

Silver, H. (2003) Does a university have a culture? *Studies in Higher Education, 28*(2), 157-169.

Srikanthan, G., & Dalrymple, J. F. (2002). Developing a holistic model for quality in higher education. *Quality in Higher Education, 8*(3), 215-224.

Stoer-Scaggs, L. Faculty model and evaluation strategies in higher education: The Ohio State University EAP. *Employee Assistance Quarterly, 6*(1), 67-73.

Sullivan, R., & Poverny, L. (1992). Differential patterns of EAP service utilization among university faculty and staff. *Employee Assistance Quarterly, 8*(1), 1-12.

Thoreson, R. W., & Hosokawa, E. P. (Eds.) (1984). *Employee assistance programs in higher education.* Springfield, IL: Charles C. Thomas.

Tierney, W. G. (1988). Organizational culture in higher education: Defining the essentials. *Journal of Higher Education, 59*(1), 2-21.

Van Maanen, J. (1996). Ethnography. In A. Kuiper and J. Juiper (Eds.), *The social science encyclopedia* (2nd ed., pp. 263-265). London: Routledge.

doi:10.1300/J490v22n03_05

Beyond Management Consultation: Partnering with Human Resources for Organizational Effectiveness

Teresa Kulper

SUMMARY. This case study explores the need for and development of enhanced management consultation in employee assistance programs (EAPs) in academe. The partners in organizational effectiveness team (POET) program created a partnership among central Human Resources (HR) specialists, EAP counselors and consulting professionals, and departmental HR professionals at The University of Iowa, that focused on the use of a systems perspective in dealing with organizational and interpersonal problems. Program structure and content as well as program evaluation is described. Examples of cases, outcomes and estimating financial impact are interwoven into the methodology of Merrill Anderson's model of bottom-line organizational development (OD) to measure the return on investment (ROI) of developing and launching a new program. doi:10.1300/J490v22n03_06 *[Article copies available for a fee from The Haworth Document Delivery Service: 1-800-HAWORTH. E-mail address: <docdelivery@haworthpress.com> Website: <http://www.HaworthPress.com> © 2006/2007 by The Haworth Press, Inc. All rights reserved.]*

KEYWORDS. Systems thinking and application, return on investment, partnerships, productivity, outcome measurement

[Haworth co-indexing entry note]: "Beyond Management Consultation: Partnering with Human Resources for Organizational Effectiveness." Kulper, Teresa. Co-published simultaneously in *Journal of Workplace Behavioral Health* (The Haworth Press, Inc.) Vol. 22, No. 2/3, 2006/2007, pp. 75-90; and: *Employee Assistance Programs in Higher Education* (ed: R. Paul Maiden and Sally B. Philips) The Haworth Press, 2006/2007, pp. 75-90. Single or multiple copies of this article are available for a fee from The Haworth Document Delivery Service [1-800-HAWORTH, 9:00 a.m. - 5:00 p.m. (EST). E-mail address: docdelivery@haworthpress.com].

Available online at http://jwbh.haworthpress.com

doi:10.1300/J490v22n03_06

INTRODUCTION

Employee assistance programs (EAPs) have been offering services related to the seven core technologies for years. Assessment and referral for individual and family problems (non-work) and work-related concerns, remain a primary area of focus within most EAPs. Services to supervisors, such as educational sessions for recognizing symptoms of a distressed employee, how to make referrals to the EAP, as well as consultative services to supervisors and managers, are a second major focus (Blair, 2002). EAPs in academe, whether internally or externally based, tend to follow this service model.

Internal EAPs are well positioned to intervene at the systems level and to influence policy-making decisions (Akabas, 1998; Buehler, & the New York State Employee Assistance Program Council of Coordinators Subcommittee on the EAP White Paper, 2002). Seventy-eight percent of university-based EAPs that belong to the International Association of Employee Assistance Professionals in Education are internally based and serve on committees in the institution (personal communication, S. Phillips, December 4, 2003).

Internal EAPs in academe place great importance on developing relationships with managers, supervisors and human resource professionals as a source of referral, as well as developing a network of champions for the EAP program on the larger campus. EAP professionals in the academic setting must demonstrate expertise in mental health and chemical dependency assessment and referral, and often demonstrate expertise in performance management, communication, conflict resolution, anger management, and stress management in the work setting. Managers, supervisors and human resource professionals often appreciate this type of expertise and many internal EAPs receive requests to provide systems level intervention in the work setting. Leadership coaching is emerging as another example area of growth for EAP programs and is valued by managers and human resource professionals (LeFave, 2002).

It is critical that EAPs in academe are able to demonstrate positive outcomes for these services (Philips, 2004). EAPs have been shown to increase productivity, decrease absenteeism and improve health (Attridge, Amaral, & Hyde, 2003). The professional literature discusses benchmarking as a valuable tool for EAPs, but there is an increasing need to demonstrate financial benefits at the local level. Outcome research and return on investment will continue to be a focus for internal academic programs (Philips).

A third focus in the EAP field is the development of key partnerships (Amaral & Attridge, 2005) to expand service delivery capabilities and to ensure that employees are being referred and treated by the appropriate providers (e.g., workLife, wellness, and disease management programs). The employee's work functioning is an integral part of the treatment plan, and EAPs must document that they are referring and marketing all relevant services the employer provides, and ensure that partners are working toward the same outcome. Internal EAPs can also partner at the systems level with other departments on campus, such as learning and development and/or organizational development (OD), to offer services related to improving culture through effective leadership, conflict resolution, team building, improving communication and formulating workplace agreements.

University internal EAP programs can further enhance their value to the organization by combining their expertise in the areas stated above and offering additional programming that extends their systemic impact (Akabas, 1998). One example is in Faculty and Staff Services, a unit of Organizational Effectiveness (OE) in The University of Iowa's Human Resources (HR) department (Figure 1). The OE mission statement is "to support a healthy, humane and competent culture." The University of Iowa WorkLife (Wellness), Learning and Development, and Faculty and Staff Services combine to support the mission of OE.

In addition to the core EAP services described earlier, Faculty and Staff Services developed an organizational consultation program in 2000 to formalize service requests from supervisors and campus HR representatives

FIGURE 1. The University of Iowa

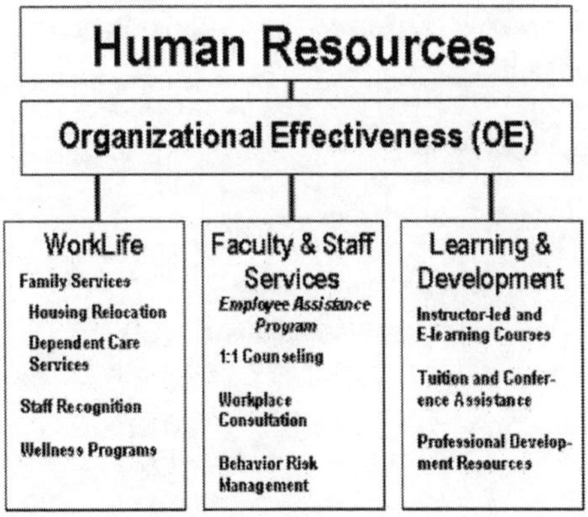

to address work group conflicts and poor communication (see Figure 2). The program relies heavily upon the action research model (Spray, 1976). Together, with the referring department's management and HR, Faculty and Staff Services partners in a systemic assessment of the situation and assists in planning appropriate interventions with stated measurable outcomes.

As requests increased beyond the capability of the existing EAP, other staff members were assigned to the organizational consultation program, which included professionals with complementary skill sets, such as a program consultant from Continuous Quality Improvement, a human resource generalist with an MBA, and the director of Learning and Development with expertise in performance management. Formalized training in organizational development and consultation assisted already systemically trained EAP counselors and others in making the transition to organizational development consultation work. By 2004, it was clear that the requests for workplace consultation would continue to outpace the staff assigned and that budget constraints would restrict hiring additional staff to meet the demands. There was also a desire on campus to push expertise out to the unit and college level where intervention has a greater chance of success to achieve savings.

FIGURE 2. The University of Iowa

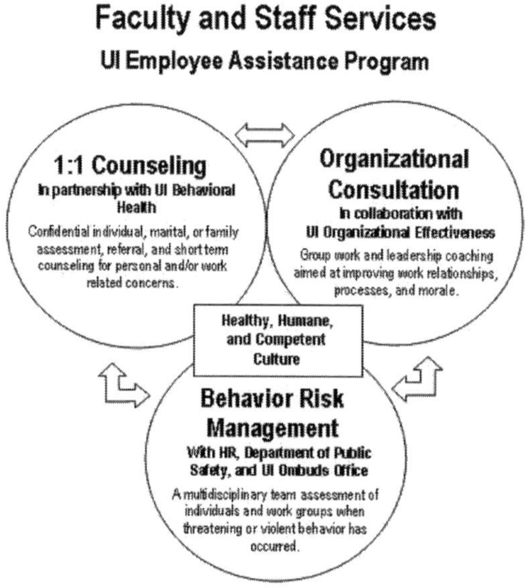

A solution to the requests/staffing dilemma and need for local expertise was found in the developing relationships with senior HR representatives who were already involved in assessment and planning services through the Faculty and Staff Services organizational consultation program. The University of Iowa central HR office and the human resources professional field in general (Ulrich & Brockback, 2005) were pressing human resources professionals to form strategic relationships with leaders, to gain a seat at the planning table rather than being seen only as policy and procedure enforcers, and to advocate for supportive and productive organizations. This resulted in the vision of partners in organizational effectiveness team (POET).

POET OVERVIEW

Faculty and Staff Services EAP professionals and workplace consultants collaborated to develop POET with The University of Iowa directors of HR and OE, and with the approval of The University of Iowa Senior Human Resources Leadership Council. The University of Iowa campus has a decentralized HR structure, with each college and major department employing its own senior human resources manager and unit representatives, responsible to their respective administration. Central HR provides centralized services such as payroll, benefits, classification and compensation, and employment services, and advice and consultation in areas such as employee and labor relations and organizational effectiveness. The Senior Human Resources Leadership Council is an advisory board to central HR.

METHODOLOGY

The directors of HR, OE and Faculty and Staff Services selected eight staff from the Senior Human Resources Leadership Council and invited them to participate in the first year of the POET program. Selections were made considering individuals' current skill sets, their stated interest in the program and their complement to the mix of people in the final group. One person dropped out early in the process as a result of scheduling conflicts, and seven successfully completed the POET program.

Merrill Anderson's bottom line organizational development model (Anderson, 2003) was selected to assist in determining the return on investment (ROI) for this initiative. This required that senior leadership develop concrete goals and 'forecast' the potential financial benefits of the POET program. Using benchmark data and anticipated benefits, it was forecasted that this initiative would have a return on investment of 338%. This was more than adequate to move forward with the project.

Long-range organizational goals for POET were: (a) to enhance the consultative and facilitative skills of senior HR representatives across campus, (b) to improve utilization and planning between departmental HR representatives and Faculty and Staff Services workplace consultants, (c) to provide specialized services, and to improve organizational effectiveness by dealing with structure, process, leadership and interpersonal issues efficiently.

Intake interviews were conducted with each of the senior HR representatives who had accepted the invitation to participate in POET. Building upon the organizational goals developed by the senior leadership, participants were asked to further develop goals and measures of success for their own areas. One mutual unit and participant goal was to have unit leadership recognize POET participants as experts in organizational effectiveness. This was achieved by enhancing participants' ability to systemically assess organizational functioning, making recommendations in ways that leadership could hear, accessing key resources, and by increasing participants' confidence to deal with issues proactively. Anticipated financial benefits from this partnership included reduced costs for conflict resolution services such as arbitration, increased productivity in the units where the services were rendered and increased productivity of the POET participants.

Research was conducted on the anticipated benefits to ultimately determine the financial value. Organization-related costs (see Table 1) were used to determine ROI at the end of the POET program.

Following the completion of the program and consistent with Anderson's (2003) model, leaders and participants were again interviewed, this time to describe specific benefits gained. Participants estimated how much of the benefit was attributable to participation in the POET program. The next step was to state how confident they were in this attribution. This two-step process provided a more conservative, and more accurate, reflection of the POET Program's ROI (see ROI section below).

Faculty and Staff Services consultants used our systems training in developing and delivering the POET program. All Faculty and Staff Services counselor/consultants were involved in planning and presenting material and in case consultations throughout the year. The intention was to value the relationship development between participants and Faculty and Staff Services staff and to assist everyone in developing expertise. The added value was in the role model of a systemic approach to program development.

POET PROGRAM STRUCTURE AND PROCESS

The POET Program was a year-long initiative starting with three half-day formal workshops followed by less-structured, monthly, case-specific roundtable meetings. Each of the three highly interactive workshops contained educational activities and lecture content, skill-building practice opportunities, tools and resources. Workshops and roundtables demonstrated clear application of systems and organizational development concepts through the use of current challenges and case examples identified by the participants or consultants.

The first workshop included a kick-off and charge from The University of Iowa director of HR, who spoke to the group about creating healthy and humane work environments, and the role of HR in improving culture. She encouraged participants to develop strong relationships with leaders so that they would be seen as crucial partners when important decisions were being made. She asked them to assist central HR by identifying ways to be more supportive and informative. Her vision was to create a communication feedback loop to insure optimal communication and resource utilization. The major training focus of this session was systems thinking and analysis. Objectives were for POET participants to be able to identify basic systems concepts and principles, to understand how systems concepts were built into the Faculty and Staff Services organizational consultation model, and to understand change and resistance to change.

One month later, the second workshop focused on resolving conflict, understanding multiple perspectives and assisting groups with communication. Objectives for this session included developing strategies and tools for addressing conflict rather than avoiding conflict and learning methods for self-care when dealing with high conflict situations.

The third workshop further honed skills in facilitating discussions and meetings. In this session, the group explored communication styles, group processes and group development. Participants worked on planning, facilitating and evaluating group meetings.

For the rest of the year the group met monthly in roundtable discussions. Participants brought challenging situations from their respective units. The group would attempt to analyze the case from a systems point of view, and form a plan for approaching the situation in a new or stronger perspective. The next month participants would report back on how the approach worked or did not work and what they intended to do next or do differently when a similar situation arises. Participants held strategic conversations about developing relationships with unit leadership, when to push for change and when to accept and work within the system. While only one or two cases could be covered in a month, participants regularly commented on how applicable the discussions were to situations in their unit. This helped them better prepare for situations that may arise. Faculty and Staff Services EAP counselor/consultants would identify appropriate EAP referral opportunities and provide language for referring leaders and employees to the EAP if red flags were raised. An added benefit to the larger organization was the guidance related to organizational system functioning.

One case example involved a departmental leader who was perceived as particularly demanding and had extremely high expectations of his support staff. Over a two-year period, there was a high turnover of four secretaries who reported to him. His current secretary had transferred from another department according to union contract and he was unhappy about the mandatory hire, even though she had the necessary skill and knowledge and was quite competent, according to prior performance reviews. When the time came to write performance reviews, he gave her extremely low scores with very cutting remarks. In a routine process, the Human Resources representative/POET participant reviewed the appraisal prior to the employee receiving it. She could foresee that the employee's response to the appraisal might result in a formal grievance or a complaint to the University ombudsperson. Despite the fact that she had had previous meetings with the departmental leader about his staffing problems, and his inability to see that his leadership style may be contributing to the problems, the HR representative contacted him to discuss the situation. She had him estimate how much time he was spending training new secretaries, how much work he had to do when he had no secretary and what he really needed from his support staff. Eventually, he was able to see his concerns and goals in the context of the larger system. Consequently, they rewrote the evaluation together with honest feedback about what he wanted the employee to do differently, in positive terms, and with focus on the future. The HR representative checked with the leader after a few months and he reported the working relationship with his secretary had improved.

POET OUTCOMES

As outlined in Methodology, each participant was interviewed post-program. They were asked to list specific outcomes of the cases they had impacted over the year. A dollar figure for those outcomes was assigned based on the organization-related costs (see Table 1). POET participants listed several positive outcomes (see Table 2 for a summary). In one situation, the participant's unit won arbitration, in another they avoided a grievance and in two situations, the participants believed they had avoided lawsuits. It was very interesting to note the savings related to reducing conflict in an area. For example, in one situation several faculty and staff were very upset with the administrator of their area. They would complain to each other, come to the HR representative/POET participant to complain, and have meetings without the administrator there to talk about what to do. With assistance from a Faculty and Staff Services consultant and the POET group, the HR representative began to get people to talk to the administrator, the dean began to hold the administrator accountable to a performance improvement plan and the administrator began leadership coaching. Eventually the work group was reorganized with more efficient workflow. The POET participant estimated that the hours spent weekly decreased from 10 hours per week to 5 hours per week at a cost avoidance of $21,000 over a three-month period alone. Many of the POET participants commented on how they were able to save meeting time by requesting that all of the people involved in a particular decision or conflict be at the same table at the same time, and that good facilitation enabled the group to arrive at a conclusion more efficiently. Another cost avoidance outcome was in reducing unnecessary turnover; in four situations the POET participant believed that turnover was avoided by the systems-based intervention.

In addition to cost-avoidance benefits, participants noted increases in the productivity of their workgroups and leaders. For example one participant noted that her direct boss was able to spend much less time investigating complaints, coaching his supervisory staff and trying to motivate the workforce. She estimated his productivity was up by 10% due to more timely and efficient approaches to problems. Four of the

TABLE 1. Organization-Related Costs

Average cost of third-step grievances		
Employee & Labor Relations, 2 hrs		$70
Department Manager, 1 hr		35
Department HR Representative, 2 hrs		70
Supervisor, 2 hrs		70
Union Steward, 2 hrs		48
Employee, 2 hrs		48
	Total	**$341**
Average cost of arbitration		
Employee & Labor Relations, 8 hrs		$280
Department Manager, 8 hrs		280
Department HR Representative, 8 hrs		280
Supervisor, 8 hrs		280
Union Steward, 4 hrs		96
Employee, 4 hrs		96
UI portion of Arbitrators' fee ($4,000/2)		2000
Cost of third-step grievance (above)		341
	Total	**$3,653**
Est. average cost of lawsuit settled out of court		
Potential savings accrued per case		**$16,000**
(The University of Iowa General Counsel)		
Average cost of turnover		**$50,000**
Source: Bradley, M. *HR metrics: A five step approach to justifying an HR project.* Virtual presentation, June 15, 2005.		
Average cost of dispute resolution involving UI Ombudspersons Office		
Ombudsperson, 10 hrs		$350
HR Representative, 2 hrs		70
Supervisor, 3 hrs		105
Employee, 3 hrs		105
	Total	**$630**
Cost basis		
Averages per hour, per employee group (including benefits)		
Merit Staff (hourly, contract-covered classifications)		$24
Professional and Scientific staff		35
Faculty (clinical and non-clinical)		68
Productivity per year in dollars = roughly 2 times salary		
Formula = (Hourly salary x 2) x number of hours saved		
Source: Hunter, J.E., Schmidt, F.L., & Jackson, G.B.(1982). *Meta-Analysis Cumulating Research Findings Across Studies.* Beverly Hills, CA: Sage Publications.		

TABLE 2. POET Aggregate Benefits *by Category*

Benefit Type		Benefit Type Total
Won or avoided arbitration (1 case)		$3,653
Avoided grievance (1 case)		341
Group productivity (3 cases)		182,209
Avoided lawsuit (2 cases)		32,000
Resolved conflicts, saved meeting time (3 cases)		27,959
Personal productivity (4 cases)		93,272
Prevented turnover (4 cases with 6 prevented)		300,000
	Total	**$671,309**

seven participants believed their personal productivity was up 10-20% due to participation in the program.

RETURN ON INVESTMENT (ROI)

Anderson (2003) differentiates hard data from soft data and advocates that systemic change initiatives should measure both. Hard data measures are those that are objective and easy to convert into a monetary value. Since most organizations and businesses collect and make decisions based on hard data, efforts to demonstrate these types of gains carry credibility with business leaders. "Evaluating hard and soft data go hand in hand. Improved project completion (hard) may have been possible only with improved decision making (soft); improved employee productivity (hard) may be an expression of loyalty (soft); and order shipment fidelity (hard) may be an important factor in creating more satisfied customers (soft)" (Anderson).

Wellness programs and EAPs have a solid history of using both hard and soft data to measure program outcomes. As stated above, EAPs have shown positive outcomes such as improved productivity, decreased absenteeism and reduced health care costs (Attridge, 2003). Organizational development has also focused on hard data measures such as improved productivity or reducing costs (Weisbord, 1987). In teaching and applying systems thinking to the organizational units of POET participants, both the hard data (productivity and cost avoidance) as well as soft data (participants seen as experts in the field and improved coordination between participant and OE) was evaluated.

As stated above, we had forecasted the potential benefits of POET by interviewing the senior HR leadership and participants, determining the units of measurement, and costing those benefits (see Table 1). Forecasting has several benefits to a change program such as POET. ". . . the forecasting process introduces a level of discipline and business focus that leads to increasing the value of the strategic initiative" (Anderson, 2003). With forecasting, there is a clear expectation of value that is set by leadership and participants, creating mutual accountability for the success of the program. Determining up front the anticipated benefits and value of those benefits creates an environment where "everyone knows what the prize is" (Anderson, 2003) and the decision to move forward with the project is based on business impact. In many ways forecasting is a systemic activity, bringing multiple perspectives and desired outcomes to the table and creating a shared vision for the effort. This served as a role model for the kinds of systematic processes we were attempting to teach in POET.

Finally, also following Anderson's (2003) model, we attempted to isolate the effects of the POET initiative. There are several ways to determine if the benefits achieved are coming from the program being evaluated: estimate the attribution, put an error limit on the estimation, be conservative at every stage, use multiple measures where possible, consult with experts and use control groups when prudent (Anderson). For every outcome that the POET participants listed at the exit interview, they were asked, "What percent of this outcome is attributable to your involvement in POET?" The monetary value based on the organization-related cost chart (Table 1) was then decreased by that percent. The participant was then asked, "How confident are you in that attribution of benefit?" and the monetary values were again decreased by that percent. Examples of a few of the participants' estimations can be found in Table 3. To calculate POET ROI, the more conservative net benefit total was used.

To answer critics of this estimation process, Anderson offers, "Business is based on estimations, assumptions, judgment, and–truth be known–guesswork. The point here is that bottom line OD operates in a business environment, follows the same standards, and uses the same financial tools. This approach is not perfect to be sure, but it places the change practitioner on the same playing field, playing by the same rules as other business-people, which is a good thing" (Anderson, 2003). Frank Schmidt, PhD, reviewed our program and the method used in Table 3, and agreed that attempting to qualify the monetary benefits outweighs any concerns about the use of estimation (F. L. Schmidt, personal interview, February 17, 2006).

TABLE 3. POET Aggregate Benefits Attribution Detail

2 examples, by benefit type

Benefit Type	$ value	Attributed to POET	% of Confidence	Net $	Benefit Type Total
Resolved conflicts, saved meeting time					
Resolved raise	4,240	75%	90%	2,862	
Less time on conflicts	21,000	60%	100%	12,600	
Saved meeting time	2,343	50%	50%	586	
Saved meeting time	376	70%	70%	184	
Totals	**$27,959**				**$16,232**
Prevented turnover					
Prevented turnover	50,000	60%	100%	30,000	
Prevented turnover	50,000	85%	90%	38,250	
Prevented turnover × 3	150,00	60%	80%	72,000	
Prevented turnover	50,000	85%	90%	38,250	
Totals	**$300,000**				**$178,500**

The POET program's aggregate monetary benefits totaled $318,874 after reducing the amount according to attribution and confidence levels. This translates to $45,553 per participant. The final step in determining ROI was to calculate costs and plug benefits and costs into an ROI formula ROI = (benefits-costs)/cost x 100.

The costs of POET were fairly high. As stated above, to model systems thinking and to support the relationships being developed in the program, all Faculty and Staff Services counselors and consultants participated in every workshop and roundtable discussion. Faculty and Staff Services staff spent 50 hours in design and development of the workshops at a cost of $2250, using the average hourly salary of a professional and scientific employee, noted in Table 1. Including costs of intake interviews brought the development costs to $2625. Deployment of the program, including food and travel and exit interviews, again using average hourly salaries, cost $6885. Opportunity costs were $2124. Total program costs were $14,870 or $2124 per participant.

In summary of POET program ROI, the benefits were $318,874; the costs were $14,870. ROI = (benefits, $318,874-costs, $14,870)\costs, $14,870 × 100 = 2044%. To be extra conservative, ROI was cut in half (a common practice, according to Anderson), and still the program is seen as successful and worth repeating (M. C. Anderson, personal communication, April 26, 2006).

FUTURE CONSIDERATIONS

This program was a learning process for everyone involved. Determining financial benefits is not easy and invites debate. The more campus experts involved in the debate strengthened the project as well as got others interested in doing this for their programs and initiatives. While ROI was very high for this program, it is uncertain if similar benefits will be achieved in year two and following years. Was it the particular mix of participants? Was it the excitement of Faculty and Staff Services staff in developing and deploying the program that created such good outcomes? Even without publicizing the financial outcomes, the program is very popular, with additional HR representatives asking to be involved in subsequent years.

The soft data is equally important to the ROI. The validation and support of the case management process was invaluable to participants and consultants but not considered in the financial outcomes reported above. Other intangibles reported by participants include increased confidence and improved respect from their deans and managers. Participants also felt more confident about when to call Faculty and Staff Services for specialized services and what to expect from those services. One participant stated she believed that the reputation of the college she represented was improved when employees were less disgruntled and turnover was avoided. Participants appreciated the feeling that they had a better tool box for dealing with difficult situations.

While systems training and understanding human behavior and motivation provide a great background for this type of work, EAP professionals can also benefit from additional training in business and organizational development. Formal training is helpful; the informal learning that comes from partnering with others is invaluable. Faculty and Staff Services counselors and consultants found that the exchange of ideas and development of case plans in the moment created an exciting learning environment for all.

One challenge in this type of management consultation is in managing the data. The ROI study asked for data that Faculty and Staff Services did not normally track which meant having to go back and create systems for tracking the important data elements. The other challenge is generating the data of partners who may not track or store the data needed. Faculty and Staff Services consultants created a worksheet for future POET participants to use to track active cases. While it was relatively easy to remember the cases that participants discussed in roundtable meetings, there were possibly other cases that participation in POET influenced but the participant had forgotten by the time of the exit interviews.

This program has caused Faculty and Staff Services and OE leaders to redouble their efforts in partnerships across campus. Academe is a special environment with multiple stakeholders in organizational effectiveness. Partnerships can strengthen programs, reduce redundancy and make use of complementary skill sets.

ACKNOWLEDGMENTS

The authors would like acknowledge Pat Kenner, Carol Wozniak-Rebhuhn, Joan Rinner and Nikole Mac for their contributions to the POET program and this article. Thanks also to Susan Buckley and Laura Reed for their vision and support of POET and their contributions to this article.

REFERENCES

Akabas, S. (1998). Employee assistance programs. *Encyclopedia of Occupational Health and Safety. Geneva: ILO.*

Amaral, T., & Attridge, M. (2005, October). *Expanding EAP Business Value through Strategic Partnerships: A Review of Research and Best Practices.* Paper presented at the Employee Assistance Professionals Association National Conference, Philadelphia, PA.

Anderson, M. C. (2003). *Bottom-line organization development: Implementing and evaluating strategic change initiatives for lasting value.* Burlington, MA: Butterworth-Heinemann/Elsevier.

Attridge, M., Amaral, T., & Hyde, M. (2003). Completing the business case for EAPs. *Journal of Employee Assistance, 33*, 23-25.

Blair, B. (2002).Consultative services: Providing added value to employers. *Exchange, 32*, 21-23.

Buehler, D. L., & the New York State Employee Assistance Program Council of Coordinators Subcommittee on the EAP White Paper. (2002, September 17). *The Competitive Advantage of Internal EAPs.* Retrieved November 2, 2006, from the International Association of Employee Assistance Professionals in Education Web site: http://www.iaeape.org/whitepaper.pdf

LeFave, A. (2002). Competency-based coaching: Drawing on traditional EA skills. *Exchange, 32*, 26-27.

Philips, S. B. (2004). Client satisfaction with university employee assistance programs. *Employee Assistance Quarterly, 19*, 59-70.

Spray, S. L. (1976). *Organizational effectiveness: Theory, research and application.* Kent, Ohio: Kent State University.

Ulrich, D. & Brockback, W. (2005). *The HR value proposition.* Boston: Harvard Business School Press.

Weisbord, M. R. (1987) *Productive workplaces revisited: Dignity, meaning and community in the 21st century.* San Francisco: Jossey-Bass, Inc.

doi:10.1300/J490v22n03_06

University Employee Assistance Program Response to Traumas on Campus

Andrew Silberman
James W. Kendall
Amanda L. Price
Theodore A. Rice

SUMMARY. When trauma affects a University workforce, health and productivity are compromised, and an organized response can help lessen the emotional impact and accelerate recovery of function. Responding to traumatic events in the workplace has evolved into being the responsibility of many EAPs. The authors present how the Critical Incident Stress Management (CISM) model was adapted by their internal EAPs in academic settings at Duke and Vanderbilt to help manage the psychological and occupational ramifications of critical incidents. Outcome data generated from evaluation of Duke's program is presented, which demonstrates the value of the interventions in helping employees

Andrew Silberman and Amanda Price, Duke Personal Assistance Service, Duke University; James Kendall and Theodore Rice, Vanderbilt University.

For their significant roles in developing CIRP at Duke, authors thank Muki Fairchild, LCSW, Elizabeth Stewart, MSN and Linda Jordan, PhD; and for their significant help. Undeveloping VCISM at Vanderbilt, authors thank Ellen Trice, LCSW, Donna L. Buehler, MSSW and Mary Yarbrough, MD, MPH.

Correspondence concerning this article should be addressed to Andrew Silberman, Duke Personal Assistance Service, Duke University Medical Center, Box 3834, Durham, NC 27710.

[Haworth co-indexing entry note]: "University Employee Assistance Program Response to Traumas on Campus." Silberman, Andrew, et al. Co-published simultaneously in *Journal of Workplace Behavioral Health* (The Haworth Press, Inc.) Vol. 22, No. 2/3, 2006/2007, pp. 91-109; and: *Employee Assistance Programs in Higher Education* (ed: R. Paul Maiden and Sally B. Philips) The Haworth Press, 2006/2007, pp. 91-109. Single or multiple copies of this article are available for a fee from The Haworth Document Delivery Service [1-800-HAWORTH, 9:00 a.m. - 5:00 p.m. (EST). E-mail address: docdelivery@haworthpress.com].

Available online at http://jwbh.haworthpress.com

doi:10.1300/J490v22n03_07

manage reactions and in the restoration of personal and occupational functioning. A survey conducted by the authors provides an overview "snapshot" of the active roles that University EAPs have currently in responding to workplace traumas. The survey results underscore the importance of developing a coordinated response and using trained responders, and of the need for additional evaluation of interventions to determine effectiveness of response. doi:10.1300/J490v22n03_07 *[Article copies available for a fee from The Haworth Document Delivery Service: 1-800-HAWORTH. E-mail address: <docdelivery@haworthpress.com> Website: <http://www.HaworthPress.com>*

KEYWORDS. Critical incident, EAP, university, trauma response, workplace, CISM, psychological first aid, survey, evaluation

INTRODUCTION

When trauma occurs in any organization, health and productivity are compromised. Any number of traumatic events or critical incidents can affect the functioning of faculty and staff in an academic setting with a medical center. A "critical incident" is defined as an event that has the potential to overwhelm one's usual coping mechanisms resulting in psychological distress and an impairment of normal adaptive functioning (Everly & Mitchell, 1999). A few examples of critical incidents in the academic and health center workplace include: line of duty death, suicide or homicide of employee, mass casualties, hostage situation, natural disasters resulting in severe injury/death or destruction, and workplace violence in which life is threatened. Critical incidents create significant disruptions throughout an organization and evoke a wide range of cognitive, behavioral, and emotional reactions for those who experience or witness them. Employees reeling from a critical incident frequently become less productive, experience absenteeism, are at risk for an increase in accidents, and at higher risk for behavioral and emotional readjustment difficulties. Health care costs can rise and turnover of staff is not unusual.

The Critical Incident Response Program (CIRP) at Duke University and the Critical Incident Stress Management Response Program (VCISM) at Vanderbilt University are structured, organized responses that provide early intervention services and support to those who have experienced a critical incident. CIRP is co-directed by the internal EAP, Personal Assistance Service, at Duke University in Durham North Carolina.

The VCISM is coordinated through Work/Life Connections-EAP, the employee assistance program at Vanderbilt University in Nashville Tennessee. Both of these EAPs are internal, in academic settings with large medical centers and an extensive health system complex with specialized level I trauma centers, and have over 45,000 faculty and employees combined. There have been a number of critical incidents each year that have affected the emotional well-being and productivity of the University community. The response programs at Duke and Vanderbilt were developed in part to provide specialized intervention for these events that are so powerful and extraordinary that normal coping skills fail, and are part of their University's disaster plans and integral in the various sub-plans. Both programs have adapted the CISM model as the foundation for their response programs.

In 1983, Jeffrey Mitchell introduced the CISD, critical incident stress debriefing, to support rescue personnel following a particularly powerful and emotionally charged event which negatively impacted the functioning of first responders. The "Mitchell Model" utilized mental health professionals along with "peer debriefers" (trained fire fighters, police officers and paramedics) to provide emotional first aid in a psychoeducational group setting. It was designed for homogeneous workgroups (police, fire and EMS). He used "peer debriefers" to assist mental health facilitators by "translating" the rescue jargon and increasing the credibility and acceptance of the process in a traditionally closed culture (Mitchell, 1983). Later, CISD was renamed "CISM," critical incident stress management, to more accurately reflect the multi-dimensional aspect of this crisis intervention system.

One of the key benefits of workplace trauma interventions is to provide the work community a structure to interpersonally process the impact of a shocking event. The core components of CISM provide a structured process for delivering psychological first aid. Critical Incident Stress Management is not psychotherapy, nor is it intended for use as an intervention to mitigate the effects of chronic stress or repeated exposure to a stressful work environment. The CISM intervention techniques taught by the International Critical Incident Stress Foundation (ICISF) provide a framework for response to individuals and groups impacted by a traumatic event.

Leadership and management in the organization can feel overwhelmed when responding to the myriad details and demands posed by a critical incident, and may feel at a loss as to how to respond appropriately or effectively to support themselves and their employees. Secondary victimization can result when there is a lack of appropriate response to traumas in the workplace. This occurs when there is denial of necessary services by leadership, minimization of the magnitude of the incident, or lack of understanding among those in the organization about the impact of trauma on cognitive, emotional and physical functioning. In such situations, people's reactions can get dismissed, misunderstood, or not responded to in appropriate ways, creating more traumas for those individuals. In addition, group support in the aftermath of a workplace trauma is not always spontaneous. Due to disruption of usual group process and individual functioning, significant barriers to the mobilization of group support may arise. Furthermore, the organizational culture of the workplace may mitigate against the support and communication necessary to address the trauma (Braverman, 1992).

Determining what may be an effective response to critical incidents in the workplace is extremely important to understanding and managing reactions, restoration of functioning for the individuals involved, and restoring equilibrium for the organization as a whole.

The Components of CISM Include:

1. **Pre-incident education:** Information about stress resilience training, available support services and accessing response following traumas or disasters.
2. **1:1 supportive contacts:** Supportive counseling contacts provided to an individual who is dealing with stress following a trauma.
3. **Defusing:** A small group technique to be provided within hours of the incident to those who experienced a traumatic event. The goal is assessment, triaging, acute symptom mitigation, and providing stress management information to the participants. In some cases, this intervention alone is sufficient to provide a needed sense of emotional closure.
4. **Debriefing:** A seven-step psycho-educational group process model designed to mitigate acute symptoms, create a support structure, and begin work toward psychological closure. It is particularly effective for homogeneous groups who have experienced a trauma during the performance of their jobs. It is provided between one to fourteen days following an incident and the intervention usually takes one to three hours.
5. **Crisis management briefings (CMB):** A large group intervention providing information, rumor control, and creating a sense of community support (Everly, 2000).

6. **Demobilization:** Ongoing structured emotional support at a large scale prolonged disaster or event.
7. **Follow-up/referrals:** This is part of each of the CISM techniques. There needs to be a mechanism to link participants with additional resources, such as mental health treatment beyond crisis intervention when indicated.
8. **System supports:** Organizational consultation, family interventions, and pastoral care.

EVOLUTION OF THE RESPONSE PROGRAMS

Prior to CIRP, the EAP at Duke was the sole provider for post-trauma psychological response, but at least one critical incident had exceeded its resource capacity. Although at that time there was an outpouring of support and offers of assistance from other health care providers, the well-intentioned response was fragmented and created a less optimal response. There was a lack of structure and central organizing focus, and those offering to assist had varying levels of experience or training in trauma response. This, in part, precipitated discussions about developing a comprehensive and coordinated response program that would have additional personnel who would be trained from a common model, in order to respond in a consistent manner to critical incidents. The development of Duke's CIRP was a collaborative partnership spearheaded by the directors of the EAP, departments of Social Work and Advanced Practice Nursing, and the Unicorn Bereavement Center. Pastoral Services was also involved in initial planning.

The CIRP leadership team spent a year developing the program, writing a business plan, meeting with key leaders in the organization to obtain support, designing procedures and arranging training for responders. Leadership training was conducted to promote understanding of the model. All mental health and peer counselors selected for CIRP received thirty-two hours of CISM training. Prior to program launch, internal publicity about CIRP communicated availability of this resource to the Duke community. Since then, the CIRP co-directors have presented to leadership and various managerial groups to provide summary of outcome results, and have utilized University communications to maintain visibility.

The VCISM/Trauma Response Program at Vanderbilt began out of the Employee Assistance Program in 1995. The VCISM initially responded to sporadic traumatic workplace events as the program was being established.

One of the first major tests of the Vanderbilt CISM response occurred on April 16, 1997, when an F-3 tornado ripped through downtown Nashville. Thirty-seven members of the Vanderbilt community received emotional support and tangible financial assistance. In 1998, several career ending events involving physicians came to the attention of the Medical Board due to CISM interventions. This resulted in the creation of a focused Faculty and Physician Wellness Program within Work/Life Connections-EAP.

Three years later the tragic events of September 11 provided the next milestone solidifying CISM as a part of the University infrastructure. The University Disaster Committees placed mental health counselors at multiple locations anticipating a flood of traumatized students, patients, families and staff. The CISM Advisory Team coordinated the supportive response for the Vanderbilt community and provided information on coping with trauma, 1:1 support, group psycho-educational activities, and coordinated communication updates to administration concerning the counseling efforts on campus. Over four hundred members of the Vanderbilt community received some form of support in September 2001. This formalized the Work/Life Connections-EAP office as the central conduit for campus traumatic event support.

PROGRAM GOALS

The goals of the Response Programs are to have CISM trained teams available to:

1. Lessen the impact of trauma
2. Reduce feelings of isolation
3. Accelerate recovery of function
4. Enhance personal resources and support systems
5. Assess for further intervention/support
6. Attempt to help prevent long-term mental health consequences

DELIVERY OF SERVICES

Following a critical incident at Duke, one of the CIRP co-directors is contacted. After consulting with the management of the unit(s) involved, the co-directors confer to discern what type of response may be helpful and begin formulating an intervention plan to address the particular incident and the needs of the population affected. Adaptation and accommodation of specific interventions to fit the particular circumstances are essential to most effectively assist faculty and staff following a critical incident (Everly & Mitchell, 1999; Everly & Mitchell, 2000). A CIRP team leader is assigned and a response team is organized from the list of trained responders. Those who experienced or witnessed the critical incident are invited to meet. Members of the response team and the co-director provide follow-up for those who may need additional assistance or support beyond the interventions. Evaluation is conducted via questionnaire two weeks post-intervention for both the participants and the manager.

At Vanderbilt, Work/Life Connections-EAP provides the infrastructure and leadership role within the university coordinating the crisis management model. The CISM Team has also anticipated the potential need to respond to larger critical incidents and has partnered with hospitals in the Middle Tennessee area. The manager of the EAP is the team coordinator, given his extensive expertise with Crisis Intervention techniques. Key representatives from a variety of areas on campus form a CISM Advisory Board, including: EAP, Pastoral Care, Chaplains, Social Services, the Mental Health Center, the Counseling Center, Student Health, the Medical School, the Women's Center, Student Housing and the Psychiatric Hospital. The CISM Team is accessed through a call tree protocol with the initial call going to the EAP office for triage assessment. The Coordinator, or designee, discusses the situation with the response initiator and determines the most appropriate intervention(s) and responder(s). Following a response to a significant event, the Advisory Board reviews the response and known circumstances surrounding the event to review a "lessons learned" document. Organizationally, this has been used to create policies, programs and training programs.

PROVIDING SPECIALIZED TRAINING

There are a number of critical incident response models (Boudreaux & McCabe, 2000; Spitzer & Burke, 1993; Weaver, Morgan, Dingman, Hong, & North, 2000). A widely recognized model for critical incident stress management is based on the work of Jeffrey Mitchell, PhD and George Everly Jr, PhD, FAPM (Everly & Mitchell, 1999; Mitchell & Hopkins, 1998). Regardless of the model used, it is imperative that responders to workplace traumas have specialized training in the provision of psychological first aid and the techniques of disaster response. Both of the Programs at Duke and Vanderbilt believed that the CISM model was best suited for a corporate and tertiary healthcare setting and have adapted it for use in their settings, with trained mental health and peer counselors comprising the response teams. Duke CIRP has trained over forty responders, while Vanderbilt CISM Team trained over ninety university mental health and nursing personnel in the techniques of CISM. Additionally, over the last five years, the Vanderbilt CISM Team provided training to over a hundred EA and mental health counselors from other hospitals in the area in preparation for a potential community-wide disaster.

ADVANTAGES OF AN INTERNAL EAP

Internal EA programs at universities are ideally positioned to intervene in workplace trauma because they are a known and trusted resource. They have established credibility with leaders on campus and in the medical center, are intimately familiar with the workplace culture, and are professionally invested in the well being of its employees. The Mitchell CISM protocol for rescue personnel emphasizes that a CISM Team responds only when requested. In contrast, an internal EAP model is positioned to encourage proactive interventions when an incident impacts the workplace. Managers often contact the EAP requesting immediate "help," some kind of response to support their employees at the awareness of a workplace fatality, or an overwhelming workplace incident. Managers don't generally know the nature of the response they need so they rely on the program to provide consultation and assistance.

The authors suggest eight key advantages of having an organized protocol for responding to traumas in the workplace.

1. **Supplies a Desired Immediate Intervention:** In times of emotional crisis, managers and organizations welcome experienced consultation and interventions that can support the needs of the workforce.
2. **Emphasizes support by the organization:** Visible interventions highlight the commitment that the organization has to supporting the emotional welfare of their employees.
3. **Outlines structure during time of high stress:** Critical incidents are by their very definition situations that have the potential to "overwhelm one's usual coping mechanisms resulting in psychological distress" and a chaotic process can result. Utilizing EAP as

a point contact provides a structured format to help managers and employees work through a difficult event.

4. **Encourages forum for dialogue:** During times of stress, many people benefit from camaraderie and openly processing their feelings. This should be voluntary.
5. **Creates formal recognition of stressful impact:** Taking time to process a traumatic event gives it recognition and importance. It behaviorally speaks to the support that an organization can offer its employees.
6. **Imparts information on stress management:** The interventions serve as an opportunity to disseminate information about typical reactions and healthy ways to manage stressful situations by emphasizing coping tools and strategies for self-care.
7. **Offers information about counseling resources:** The intervention also markets the available services of the EAP and other counseling resources that employees can access.
8. **Provides a High Visibility Intervention:** Most of the work done by an EAP is with individuals in a confidential treatment setting. Services can seem to be invisible to the organization as a whole. A CISM response reminds the constituents that there are services available to provide emotional support, and it emphasizes to the organization the importance of work done by the EAP.

PROGRAM UTILIZATION

Since formal implementation in December 2001, Duke's CIRP has received thirty-five calls about incidents. Fifteen of these were deemed to be critical incidents and were provided services through the CIRP program. The majority of other incidents were deemed not to meet the criteria as a critical incident yet still needed support and assistance. These included accidents, assault by a patient, and off-site death. In those instances, Duke's EAP and other resources such as Social Work and Bereavement Services provided consultation and services without activating the broader resources of the CIRP program.

At Vanderbilt, since 2000, there have been interventions for twenty critical incidents involving deaths of colleagues, students or family members. These have resulted in forty-two separate interventions. Five of those situations involved the suicide of a colleague, spouse or employee's child. The EAP provides psycho-educational information on grief and the availability of therapy resources. With some modifications of the CISM tools, "de-griefing" interventions for events surrounding loss can help a workgroup begin the process grief and attain emotional closure.

Program Evaluation

Program evaluation has been conducted at Duke following CIRP interventions to determine effectiveness of the interventions and the primary goals of symptom management and restoration of personal and occupational functioning. The outcome measurements have been targeted to participants in defusings and debriefings. In a departure from the traditional Mitchell model, a questionnaire is mailed to these group participants two weeks following the intervention (see Appendix A). A pre-addressed and stamped envelope is included, which allows for participants to return the questionnaire anonymously. Directors or managers who requested assistance for their work unit are mailed a separate questionnaire, two weeks after the response, to obtain their feedback about the process and effectiveness of the intervention (see Appendix B). Through February of 2006, the response rate for participants has been 36%. The managerial response rate has been 56%.

Overall, the questionnaire results from participants indicate that the CIRP interventions have been helpful and effective (see Table 1). More than two-thirds of participants reported that they felt better able to cope after the CIRP intervention (71%), and felt better prepared to return-to-work (69%). This was perhaps one of the most important findings

TABLE 1. Percentage of Responses* for CIRP Participant Evaluations

Questions	Strongly Agree	Agree	Unsure	Disagree	Strongly Disagree
1. Overall intervention helpful	40	54	6		
2. Better understood incident	26	51	3	17	3
3. Understand reactions and feelings	29	63	3	6	
4. Better able to cope	20	51	23	6	
5. Safe place to talk/listen	49	49		3	
6. Learned additional resources	32	62	6		
7. Better prepared to return to work	17	51	23	9	
8. Manager arranged time off to participate	36	52	9	3	
9. Recommend CIRP intervention	40	54	6		

* N = 35

of the outcome evaluation in support of the value of offering these interventions. Most all participants reported that they better understood their reactions following the intervention (91%) and learned about additional resources they could utilize for follow-up as needed (94%). Finally, most participants also strongly agreed or agreed that they would recommend a CIRP intervention to others who had been affected by a critical incident (94%).

The data obtained from the manager questionnaire also demonstrated that CIRP has been helpful and effective (see Table 2). The process and support provided to the manager by CIRP in helping to respond to employee needs following a critical incident has received high marks. From their perspective and observation of their employees, all the managers (100%) strongly agreed or agreed that: CIRP interventions were helpful to them in their role, had helped the staff cope better, provided staff with information and additional resources, and would utilize CIRP again in the event of another incident. Almost every manager reported that the CIRP intervention had helped staff return to their pre-incident functioning at work (90%).

TABLE 2. Percentage of Responses* for CIRP Management/Leadership Evaluations

Questions	Strongly Agree	Agree	Unsure	Disagree	Strongly Disagree
1. Easy to access	60	40			
2. Contacted in timely manner	100				
3. Adequately explained CIRP response	80	20			
4. Informed of CIRP team's plan	100				
5. Team arrived on time	100				
6. Team treated staff with respect	100				
7. Talked with manager before and after	100				
8. Intervention helped understand incident	60	20	20		
9. Intervention helped cope with incident	60	40			
10. Intervention helped return to functioning	50	40	10		
11. Provided information and resources	80	20			
12. Intervention helpful to me (manager)	80	20			
13. Would call CIRP for staff again	90	10			

* N = 10

MEASURING EFFECTIVENESS

As with most mental health interventions, meaningful outcome data concerning CISM interventions is limited. Historically the effectiveness of such interventions has been measured by self-reported improvement, utilization, participation or feedback about the satisfaction of the overall response reported by participants, managers or administration (McNally, 2004). The CISM model has been the subject of some controversy in recent years (Everly & Mitchell 2000; Groopman, 2004.) Opponents to debriefing suggest that victims may be re-traumatized, debriefing does not prevent posttraumatic stress, and that there is no conclusive evidence of its effectiveness (Bledsoe, 2003; McNally, 2004). These studies examined "single session one-on-one debriefing" rather than group techniques.

Faculty and staff who participate in CISM interventions generally report that they feel better and are informed of the available resources and EAP services as a result of the Interventions. Clinically, there has not been a standard way to measure the effectiveness of various mental health interventions including CISM using a control group and equivalent sample population. Formal evaluation of particular interventions or models remains an opportunity for additional study and focus.

SURVEY OF OTHER UNIVERSITY EAPS' TRAUMA RESPONSE

Many universities, like other businesses, have realized the importance of responding to the emotional needs of their students, faculty and staff following significant traumatic events. The services provided at Duke and Vanderbilt are representative of the way that CISM or other trauma assistance model can be incorporated into the infrastructure of a University response to campus and workplace disasters. However, in order to gauge the current and prevalent role, responsibilities, and practice that other EAPs in academic environments have in responding to workplace trauma, a survey instrument was developed and sent to the membership of the International Association of EAPs in Education (IAEAPE). IAEAPE is a non-profit association representing employee assistance providers at Universities, colleges, and other educational settings in the United States and Canada (see Appendix C). The survey queried members about their University's critical incident response program or team, the EAP role, trauma model used, process of response, and whether evaluation of intervention was conducted.

Twenty-five surveys were returned by EAPs in institutions covering 1,200 to 36,000 faculty and staff. Sixteen institutions indicated that they have a Critical Incident Response plan, program, or team. All but two institutions indicated that the EAP staff determined the response to traumatic incidents. The EAP staff frequently arranged, coordinated, and provided group interventions as well as offering one-on-one counseling, consultation with managers, and follow-up services to those affected. Only six institutions indicated that they do not provide pre-incident training about traumas in the workplace.

The survey also generated information about the model used when responding to a critical incident, the type of training staff had received, and if other resources collaborated in the response. Of the twenty-five surveys returned, eleven indicated that they use the CISM model when responding to incidents while two stated that they use a modified version of this model. Nine responses indicated that they do not use a model or don't know the model used when responding. Some of the others stated that they use a psycho-educational model, a blended model, Red Cross or NOVA models. The training of responders was predominately CISM based with sixteen EAPs reporting that their staffs were trained in this model. Other training mentioned included: Red Cross, threat assessment, resiliency, NOVA, Comprehensive Acute Traumatic Stress Management, Disaster Mental Health, and first responder. Most University EAPs reported that staff from other campus departments assist with incident responses including the Student Counseling Center, Psychiatry department, Chaplain's office, Pastoral Care, and Safety office. The Red Cross, Community Mental Health Centers, and a Behavioral Healthcare organization were resources outside the university that may also be contacted by some EAPs to help respond to critical incidents.

The survey responses indicated that very few programs conduct any formal outcome evaluation of interventions. Fifteen responses indicated that they do not perform evaluations; two did not know if evaluations were performed, two stated that they sometimes or inconsistently do evaluations, three indicated verbal or phone follow-ups, and one institution said that evaluations are conducted.

Respondents' comments about advantages to having an internal EAP respond to critical incidents included: knowledge of the culture of the organization, ability to tailor response to particular group and problem, provides opportunity for longer term follow-up, EAP staff familiarity with local providers, EAP and university seen as sensitive and responsive, employees may be more likely to seek individual help because EAP staff responds, and EAP is able to offer continued consultation to managers. Advantages to having a critical incident response plan included: reduced stress for administrators, provides various ways of getting help, reduces the stigma of asking for help, a multi-disciplinary response offers varied sources for help, provides proactive measures, and could keep more serious symptoms from escalating. Limitations reported by respondents about their current response plans, which are not coordinated and comprehensive, include: no real coordinated team or management of response, little collaboration between groups who respond, interdepartmental competition and egos which can delay response, difficulty keeping employees informed, decentralized campus so there may be a delay in response, political and financial interests can interfere with response, and no pre-incident training.

CONCLUSIONS

The integration of a Trauma Response Team into the academic workplace culture is a powerful way to support the faculty and staff of a university when they experience a critical incident or traumatic event. The Response Team needs to provide ongoing pre-trauma education so that supervisors and employees know about the service, how to access it, and understand how appropriate interventions enhance health and productivity. Given the controversy that exists about this, evaluations of interventions can help a program determine effectiveness and guide improvement. The key to a successful intervention is good training, pre-planning and experience. Programs that do not utilize a coordinated team or protocol cite many limitations in the response effort when compared to those programs that do have a coordinated plan. The Internal EAP is in a unique position to help provide a proactive response that is incorporated into the policies and procedures within the organization. Few interventions will be as welcomed or valued as those supporting faculty and staff following a workplace trauma.

REFERENCES

Bledsoe, B. E. (2003). Critical Incident Stress Management (CISM): Benefit or Risk for Emergency Services. *Prehospital Emergency Care, 7*(2), 272-79.

Boudreaux, E. D. & McCabe B. (2000). Critical incident stress management I: Interventions and effectiveness. *Psychiatric Services, 51*(9), 1095-1097.

Braverman, M. (1992). Posttrauma crisis intervention in the workplace. In J. Quick, & L. Murphy, (Eds.), *Stress and Well Being at Work* (pp. 299-316). Washington DC: American Psychological Association.

Everly, G. S., Jr. (2000). Crisis Management Briefings (CMB): Large group crisis intervention in response to terrorism, disasters, and violence. *International Journal of Emergency Mental Health, 2*(I), 53-57.

Everly, G. S., Jr, & Mitchell, J. T. (1999). *Critical Incident Stress Management (CISM): A new era and standard in crisis intervention.* Ellicott City, MD: Chevron Publishing Corporation.

Everly, G. S., Jr, & Mitchell, J. T. (2000). Critical Incident Stress Management: Advanced Group Crisis Interventions Workbook. Ellicott City, MD: Chevron Publishing Corporation.

Everly, G. S., Jr. & Mitchell, J. T. (2000). The debriefing "controversy" and crisis intervention: A review of lexical and substantive issues. *International Journal of Emergency Mental Health, 2,* 211–225.

Groopman, J. (2004, January 26). The Grief Industry: How much does crisis counseling help–or hurt? *The New Yorker Magazine.*

McNally, R. J. (2004). Psychological Debriefing Does Not Prevent Posttraumatic Stress Disorder [Electronic version]. *Psychiatric Times, 21*(4).

Mitchell, J. T. (1983). When disaster strikes. The critical incident stress debriefing process. *Journal of Emergency Services, 8,* 36-39.

Mitchell, J. T., & Hopkins, J. (1998). Critical Incident Stress Management: A New Era in Crisis Intervention. Traumatic Stress Points, 12, 6/7-10/11.

Snelgrove, T. (2005). Psychological-Educational Debriefings and Outcome Assessment: A point of view Retrieved February 13, 2006, from http://www.eastonsnelgrove.com/Articles/psychoEdu.htm

Spitzer, W. J., & Burke, L. (1993). A critical-incident stress debriefing program for hospital-based health care personnel. *Health & Social Work, 18,* 149-156.

Weaver, J. D., Morgan, J., Dingman, R. L., Hong, B. A., & North, C. S. (2000). The American Red Cross Disaster Mental Health Services: Development of a Cooperative, Single Function, Multidisciplinary Service Model. *Journal of Behavioral Health Services and Research, 27*(3), 314-320.

doi:10.1300/J490v22n03_07

APPENDIX A

Duke Critical Incident Response Program

Participant Evaluation

Approximately two weeks ago you participated in a Critical Incident Response Program (CIRP) group intervention at Duke. This intervention was offered as "emotional first aid" to assist staff in coping with a critical incident that affected their work area.

In an effort to evaluate the effectiveness of the CIRP program we would appreciate your feedback. You do not need to give your name.

Your work area ____________ Date of Critical Incident Intervention ____________

Please rank the following statements about the CIRP intervention:	Strongly Agree	Agree	Unsure	Disagree	Strongly Disagree
1. Overall, the CIRP group intervention was helpful for me.	5	4	3	2	1
2. I better understood what happened in the critical incident after participating in the CIRP group intervention.	5	4	3	2	1
3. The CIRP team helped us understand the reactions and feelings that occur after experiencing a trauma.	5	4	3	2	1
4. I felt better able to cope after participating in the group intervention.	5	4	3	2	1
5. The CIRP team established the group as a safe place to talk and/or listen.	5	4	3	2	1
6. I learned about additional resources that I could use if I need further assistance.	5	4	3	2	1
7. I felt better prepared to return to work after participating in the CIRP group.	5	4	3	2	1
8. My manager arranged for me to have the time off from my normal responsibilities so I could participate in the CIRP group intervention.	5	4	3	2	1
9. I would recommend the CIRP group intervention to others.	5	4	3	2	1

Is there anything else you would like to tell us about the CIRP group intervention?

____

____

Please return the completed Participant Evaluation to Andy Silberman, MSW, CIRP Co-Director, DUMC 3834, Durham, NC 27710 or fax to 286-1121.

APPENDIX B

The Duke Critical Incident Response Program

Management/Leadership Evaluation

Thank you for activating the CIRP Team in response to the critical incident that occurred in your area. In an effort to evaluate the effectiveness of the CIRP interventions and to collect information for future program planning, we request that you complete the form below. Please return to Andy Silberman, MSW, CIRP Director, DUMC 3834.

Briefly describe the critical incident. Include the date, time and location____________

____

____

____

How did you activate the CIRP?

____

Approximately how many staff were affected by the critical incident? ______________

Please rank the CIRP Team's response to the incident:	Strongly Agree	Agree	Unsure	Disagree	Strongly Disagree
1. It was easy to access the CIRP	5	4	3	2	1
2. One of the CIRP Directors contacted me, or a member of my management team, in a timely manner to assess the situation.	5	4	3	2	1
3. The CIRP Director adequately explained how a CIRP team could respond for the type of critical incident we experienced.	5	4	3	2	1
4. I was informed of the CIRP Team's plan within a reasonable period of time including the name of the Team Leader, and the date and time of the intervention.	5	4	3	2	1
5. The CIRP Team arrived on time as planned	5	4	3	2	1
6. The CIRP Team treated the staff with respect	5	4	3	2	1
7. The CIRP Team talked with me, or my designee, before and after the intervention.	5	4	3	2	1

APPENDIX B (Continued)

Please rank the value of the CIRP intervention for your staff:	Strongly Agree	Agree	Unsure	Disagree	Strongly Disagree
8. The CIRP intervention helped the staff better *understand* the critical incident.	5	4	3	2	1
9. The CIRP intervention helped the staff better *cope* with the critical incident.	5	4	3	2	1
10. The CIRP intervention helped my staff return to their pre-incident functioning at work.	5	4	3	2	1
11. The CIRP Team provided my staff with information and additional resources (printed materials about coping & self care, appropriate referral sources, etc.)	5	4	3	2	1
12. The CIRP intervention was helpful to me as a manager.	5	4	3	2	1
13. In the event of another Critical Incident, I would call upon the CIRP team to provide emotional first aid for my staff.	5	4	3	2	1

How did you learn about Duke's Critical Incident Response Program?

Overall how would you rate the Duke Critical Incident Response Program (please circle):

Excellent Very good Good Fair Poor

Please share with us any other thoughts, suggestions, or comments that you have about the Duke Critical Incident Response Program.____________________

____

____

____

Optional Information:

Your name and title ______________________________

Phone or pager _______________ May we call you if we have additional questions? ____

Please return the completed Management/Leadership Evaluation to Andy Silberman, MSW, CIRP Director, DUMC 3834, Durham, NC 47750 or fax to 486-5545.

APPENDIX C

Survey of Critical Incident Response Models in University EAPs

1. Does your organization have a Critical Incident Response plan, program, or team to respond to the psychological ramifications of traumatic events or critical incidents?
2. How is EAP notified when there has been an incident? Who determines the type of response?
3. Does the critical incident response follow a particular model, such as: Mitchell-Everly, Red Cross, Psychological Resiliency, etc?
4. What roles does your EAP typically have in critical incident response? (Check all that apply):

   EAP conducts pre-incident training to managers and employees about traumas in the workplace______

   EAP *arranges for* group interventions following an incident_____

   EAP *coordinates* the critical incident response interventions_______

   EAP staff *provide* the critical incident response interventions _______

   EAP offers 1:1 counseling for those who have experienced or witnessed incident______

   EAP consults with managers after an incident _______

   EAP provides follow-up services to those who have been affected_______

   Other (please explain):
5. Who provides the psychological response? (Check all that apply):

   EAP staff _________

   Other staff within the organization _________ If so, who are they?

   ____

   Organization contracts out for critical incident response services_________ If so, who is the contract with? ________________________
6. If interventions such as group defusings and debriefings are conducted by EAP and/or other staff from your organization, what training do these responders have?
7. Are evaluations conducted following the response to determine effectiveness of the intervention(s)? Yes ____ No_____
8. From your experiences at your University, what do you think are the advantages and the limitations to how the responses to critical incidents in the workplace are organized?

The Creation of a Specialized University EAP Program– A Nurse Wellness Program

James W. Kendall
Theodore A. Rice
Margie Gale
Ellen Trice
Mary I. Yarbrough

SUMMARY. This article describes the evolution and components of a specialized program focused on the needs of nurses within an academic medical center provided by the internal employee assistance program at Vanderbilt University in Nashville, Tennessee. Given the unique stressors faced by this workplace population, a Nurse Wellness Program was developed to help nurses deal with workplace and personal problems. The Nurse Wellness Program of Work/Life Connections-EAP is focused on assessment, treatment, and referral of nurses as a target population. The Work/Life Connections-EAP nurse wellness clinician serves as the champion of the Nurse Wellness Program of Vanderbilt University. doi: 10.1300/J490v21n03_08 *[Article copies available for a fee from The Haworth Document Delivery Service: 1-800- HAWORTH. E-mail address: <docdelivery@haworthpress.com> Website: <http://www.HaworthPress.com> © 2006/2007 by The Haworth Press, Inc. All rights reserved.]*

[Haworth co-indexing entry note]: "The Creation of a Specialized University EAP Program–A Nurse Wellness Program." Kendall, James W., et al. Co-published simultaneously in *Journal of Workplace Behavioral Health* (The Haworth Press, Inc.) Vol. 22, No. 2/3, 2006/2007, pp. 111-126; and: *Employee Assistance Programs in Higher Education* (ed: R. Paul Maiden and Sally B. Philips) The Haworth Press, 2006/2007, pp. 111-126. Single or multiple copies of this article are available for a fee from The Haworth Document Delivery Service [1-800-HAWORTH, 9:00 a.m. - 5:00 p.m. (EST). E-mail address: docdelivery@haworthpress.com].

Available online at http://jwbh.haworthpress.com

doi:10.1300/J490v22n03_08

KEYWORDS. EAP, Nurse Wellness Program, employee assistance program, Vanderbilt University Medical Center, Faculty and Physician Wellness Program

INTRODUCTION

Work/Life Connections-EAP, the internal EAP at Vanderbilt University, launched a specialty program, the Nurse Wellness Program (NWP) in 2002, designed to identify and treat the mental health problems faced by nurses. Vanderbilt University is an internationally recognized research university in Nashville, Tennessee. It is an independent, privately supported university and the second largest private employer based in the state. Vanderbilt has an academic medical center with a Level I trauma medical center (832 licensed beds), dedicated children's hospital, comprehensive burn center, and regional air/land medical transportation. In 1992, Vanderbilt University created a dedicated Employee Assistance Program (later renamed Work/Life Connections-EAP) which emerged out of the Occupational Health Clinic in Health and Wellness within the division of Human Resources. Over the past fourteen years, Vanderbilt University's EAP has grown from one full time employee to a staff of nearly eight full time equivalents. This paper outlines the evolution of the Work/Life Connections-EAP Nurse Wellness Program-its structure, accomplishments, outcomes, and value.

NURSING IS A STRESSFUL PROFESSION

The profession of nursing is increasingly stressful (Bratt et al., 2000). Lack of control, lack of predictability, and lack of outlets for frustration are primary factors in determining stress. These factors are embedded within the entire delivery of nursing care. In addition, specialty areas in nursing often produce specific stressors. Death and dying scenarios are the most stressful for ICU and hospice nurses, while workload and staffing issues are the most stressful for medical-surgical nurses (et al., 1990). Workload and working relationships are major stressors for community mental health nurses (Cottrell, 2000). According to a study using the Maslach Burnout Inventory, nurses consistently scored higher on burnout than any other group of healthcare professionals (MedHunters Staff, 2004). The MedHunters staff (2004) noted: On the subject of dissatisfaction, a study by the American Nurses Association found that thirty percent of nurses feel powerless to improve patient safety and care, and a whopping forty percent report job dissatisfaction. "Major life events, such as divorce, death, and changing work conditions are stressful for anyone. Aside from the chance that nurses may be experiencing these events on a personal level, they are likely to experience them vicariously through their patients on a daily basis."

As the patient-staffing ratio increases, so does the risk of burnout (Aiken et al., 2002). It is estimated that up to ninety-four percent of nurses in the United States are female. The American Psychiatric Association (2000) report women are twice as likely to suffer from depression, panic disorder, and other anxiety disorders. Depression impacts nearly ten percent of the U.S. population each year, and women are twice as likely to experience depression in their lifetime compared with men. Despite the interesting findings from the prospective Nurses' Health Study correlating stress, diazepam use and death from suicide, there have been no conclusive data in the United States revealing that nurses, as an occupation, are at a significantly higher risk of suicide than other professions. The 2002 report does caution that two specific groups of nurses (a) those with combined severe stress at home and at work and (b) those reporting minimal stress ("which may reflect denial or diagnosed depression or an association with some other unmeasured risk factor") pose a concern for excess risk for suicide. (Feskanich et al., 2002) However, according to a study conducted in the United Kingdom in 2000, the suicide rate of nurses is four times that of people working outside of the healthcare professions (Davey, 2000). Health professionals face a higher risk of addiction/dependency due to the stress of the job, their knowledge of the dosages and effects of medicine, the tendency to self-diagnose and self-prescribe, and the constant focus on other people's needs instead of their own. Nurses also have greater access and physical contact with medications. "One out of seven nurses in Tennessee will experience a problem with drugs, alcohol or a condition that impairs practice at some point in his/her career" (Tennessee Professional Assistance Program, 2006).

Issues of recruitment and retention of nurses were also of national concern (Buerhaus & Needleman, 2000). In a later 2004 survey, nurses indicated that of the four factors identified in the Buerhaus et al. (2000) study, the leading recommendation on resolving the nursing shortage was to improve the work environment. The other three factors were to improve salaries and benefits, create more career options for women, and modify undesirable work hours (Buerhaus et al., 2006).

IDENTIFIED NEEDS OF NURSES AT VANDERBILT

The clinical cases involving nurses in Work/Life Connections-EAP and other organizational trends suggested that there were some unique stressors faced by nurses. Nurses acknowledged professional stressors but often could not break away from the bedside in order to attend stress management workshops or individual EAP appointments. Many nurses feel unable to take their lunch breaks or tend to personal business, such as making doctor appointments or responding to calls from their children's schools within their shifts. Twelve-hour shifts and overtime add to fatigue. Based on EAP client presenting problems, nurses were struggling with balancing the demands between work and home. The Director of Health and Wellness had already developed a successful and well respected specialized program within the EAP that focused on the professional and organizational issues faced by physicians and faculty. This Faculty and Physician Wellness Program provided a well established and credible paradigm for serving other target populations. Offering this model, expertise, and funding, the groundwork was laid for consideration of a target program for nurses within Work/Life Connections-EAP in Health and Wellness.

During that same time, over 550 Vanderbilt University Medical Center (VUMC) employees completed a Quality of Work Life Survey in 1999. The surveys were all anonymous and usually administered during public gatherings and staff meetings to provide pulse sample. Although this survey was not limited to nurses, the data were consistent with other sources of nurse feedback suggesting the following areas for improvement: a centralized employee resource center, flexible/alternate work schedules, financial incentives to reward wellness activities and healthy lifestyles, dependent care, safety, and better communication regarding the availability of existing services. In 2000, a nursing recruitment and retention initiative began, in order to address VUMC's need to attract quality nurses, retain the talented nurses currently practicing at Vanderbilt, and to create a method to monitor nurses' job satisfaction levels. The initiative was called Be the Best . . . Keep the Best. The Vanderbilt University Chief Nursing Officer recognized that balance between working and spending time at home is incredibly important for the staff and leadership. This quality of work-life includes reduced stress, a safe work environment, a manageable workload, and balanced professional and personal lives ("VUMC works," 2002).

In the same frame, Work/Life Connections-EAP was conducting an analysis of its service usage. Data indicated that only about two percent of Vanderbilt University Medical Center (VUMC) nurses utilized the EAP services compared with a four percent utilization rate by VUMC physicians and a five percent utilization rate by VUMC faculty and staff. Nurses reported that they were feeling very stressed and could not get away from the bedside to attend stress management lectures or to seek available health and wellness services. The EAP data punctuated the idea that a wellness initiative for nurses was needed.

VANDERBILT'S NEED FOR A NURSE WELLNESS PROGRAM

The Employee Assistance field has evolved significantly since the "Thundering 100" began in the 1940s focused on occupational labor movements with the alcoholic employee, the formation of the ALMCA (Association of Labor Management Administrators & Consultants on Alcoholism), followed by the introduction of managed care bringing greater inclusion of mental health issues into the labor arena. ALMACA morphed into EAPA (Employee Assistance Professionals Association) in 1989. Mental health providers and managed care companies joined internal EAPs with expanded services including trauma response and work-life programs.

In 2000, the conditions at Vanderbilt were opportune for the development of a specialized program focused on the needs of nurses. Three critical components were present allowing for the formation of this program.

A Quality Internal EAP

Vanderbilt had a seasoned EAP that served faculty and staff. The program provided traditional employee assistance services including counseling, a workplace monitoring system for employees in recovery, and a critical incident stress management program supporting staff following traumatic events in the workplace. However, the most significant factor for acceptance within the Medical Center was the success of the Faculty and Physician Wellness Program which came about in 1999. One of the most important aspects of the EAP is the division of counseling that recognizes two clients: the individual employee and the organization. Work/Life Connections-EAP provides services in three related areas.

Individual counseling. On an individual basis, there is a need to intervene and assess, counsel, or refer when the health of an employee is impaired by mental health issues such as depression, stress, or addictions. This is a key function of all employee assistance programs.

Workplace outreach. Another aspect of the EAP at Vanderbilt is the strength of its Critical Incident Stress Management (VCISM). The EAP has responded to a number of traumatic events impacting nursing staff, including the deaths of patients, colleagues, and other critical incidents. These interventions added credibility and greater exposure for the supportive services of the EAP.

Organizational Wellness Promotions. Promoting emotional wellness by encouraging appropriate ways of reducing stress through psychoeducational workshops (stress resilience, dealing with change, handling anger, challenging communications, etc.) has proven to be an effective method of marketing. Faculty and staff who are not in need of individualized assistance benefit from this skill development approach. Work/Life Connections-EAP also impacts the workplace environment through participation with university committees. These committees include: Nurse Wellness Committee, Quality of Work/life Task Force, Violence Against Women Task Force, Faculty and Staff Hardship Fund Committee, and the University Staff Advisory Board.

A SUCCESSFUL MODEL FOR SPECIALIZED TARGET POPULATION

In 1999, the Director of Health and Wellness formed a Faculty and Physician Wellness Program (FPWP), due to a grassroots task force of physicians responding to several career ending events involving physicians and faculty. The program was housed out of Work/Life Connections-EAP as it provided an existing infrastructure that confidentially assists in resolution of personal problems that impact the workplace including behavioral, emotional, relationship and addiction. One of the key components in creating the FPWP was the employment of a psychiatrist providing services based on the idea of peer-peer interaction. This move proved crucial in gaining physician acceptance for the program. Utilization by its target population, faculty and physicians employed by Vanderbilt University, increased from less than one percent to more than four percent utilization within the first five years of the inception of the Faculty and Physician Wellness Program.

A Grassroots Initiative and Support

A nurse consultant who was well respected by nurses on both a staff and administrative level was commissioned by the VUMC Chief Nursing Officer to conduct a needs assessment for Nurses and to examine the quality of the work environment for nurses. Multiple interviews with key decision makers and bedside staff nurses were conducted to gather opinions on the needs to improve the quality of work environment. This grassroots interest shown by the nursing division of VUMC identified a number of initiatives, including support for a specialty program within the Work/Life Connections-EAP focused on the professional and personal needs of nurses.

PARTNERING OF EAP WITH THE NURSE WELLNESS COMMITTEE

In 2000, six sub-groups were launched to accomplish the *Be the Best* initiative, including the creation of the Nurse Wellness Committee (NWC). The creation of a specialized Nurse Wellness Program similar to the Faculty and Physician Wellness Program was embraced. A structural component of the FPWP was the reporting of trends to an Advisory Committee. Similarly, the NWP reports to the NWC in an advisory capacity reporting case trends and aggregate data in order to impact policy and improve working conditions for nurses.

One EAP case involved a nurse who was eating her lunch at the patient bedside, which resulted in disciplinary action. She reported that there was not enough time to eat lunch or use the restroom, let alone take the required breaks. Such EAP cases, presented anonymously, serve to illuminate issues that impact nurses. Working as a member of the NWC, the manager of Work/Life Connections-EAP developed a coping with stress promotions. In November 2002, the *Take Your Break* (Figure 1) campaign was launched, recognizing that nurses are notorious for not taking shift breaks (Rogers et al., 2004). The NWC set a goal of encouraging nurses to take a few minutes of quiet time daily, changing the nursing culture and encouraging nurses to view a twelve hour shift as a marathon, not a sprint. The campaign also sought to educate nurses on the principle that breaks will increase their productivity and ability to cope with stress.

Providing stress resilience tools through in-services and unit boards is another proactive health promotions method used. In these outreach

FIGURE 1. Take Your Break

presentations on stress, it was noted that smokers manage to take a break at least once during the day allowing them to get off the unit for a few moments, socialize with colleagues and get a change of scenery. This is not to suggest that one should take up smoking. However, it does point out that nurses can take a break to use the restroom, get a snack, or take a short walk. The VUMC nurse campaign effort was highlighted and publicized by the California-based nursing website: www.nursezone.com.

When you are
running the
Nursing
Marathon
IT'S IMPORTANT TO...
...take
your
break!
sponsored by The Nurse Wellness Committee

The following are three examples of Work/Life Connections-EAP partnering with the Nurse Wellness Committee of Vanderbilt University:

Awareness Fair

The NWC sponsors an annual Nurse Wellness Fair to promote and support existing campus resources. The Nurse Wellness Program of Work/Life

Connections-EAP is active in planning and conducting this event. A number of internal programs set up promotional displays spotlighting their programs and helping to educate nurses on the many services available to them ranging from counseling, exercise, pastoral care, childcare, medical care, recreation, human resource benefits to lactation rooms, cosmetic services, and campus errand valet services.

Safety Walk

The NWC sponsored a safety walk through the Vanderbilt University campus and its medical center at night with committee members, staff nurses and safety officials to determine needs for lighting, mirrors, and other safety suggestions. Within a month, additional safety lights and mirrors were installed and tree limbs and shrubbery were trimmed. A few months later, based upon feedback from staff, the outside hospital entrances were locked at night so that visitors would enter and register in the main lobby.

Smooth Moves

Additionally, the NWC provided strong support for an initiative out of the Occupational Health Clinic called *Smooth Moves: You watch my back . . . I'll watch yours*, with a goal of decreasing staff injury and provide safe patient handling. Designated nurses, trained in the Smooth Moves protocol, provide ongoing training and expertise for each of their units. VUMC has recently approved the purchase of a number of mechanical lifting devices and patient handling aids to assist nurses in safely moving patients without causing injury to themselves.

COMPONENTS OF THE NURSE WELLNESS PROGRAM AT VANDERBILT

Work/Life Connections-EAP hired a nurse specialist to champion the NWP and provide nurse to nurse counseling services. In May 2002, the NWP was launched with the mission of connecting nurses with resources when life is challenging (Figure 2). The components of the Nurse Wellness Program include counseling, workplace outreach, and promoting wellness.

FIGURE 2

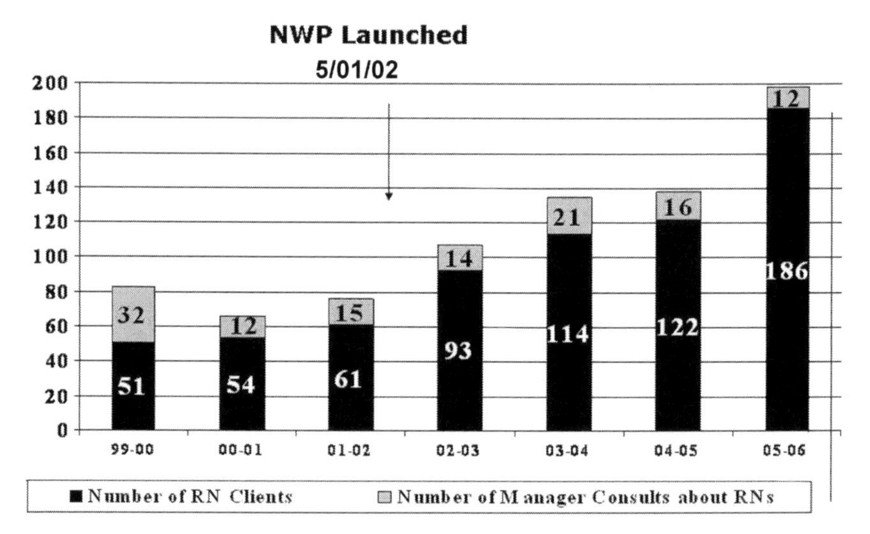

Counseling

Intervention is necessary when the emotional health of a nurse is impaired. Intervention services for the nurse include assessment, brief counseling, recovery support, community service referrals, and critical incident stress management. Nurses present to the NWP either as a self referral or as a mandatory referral. Nurse managers may suggest the use of the service or provide information as an available resource.

Depression, stress, relationship problems, parenting, eldercare, and workplace concerns are addressed through brief counseling by the EAP and referral to the community. In the case of domestic violence, the EAP counselor provides education, counseling, safety plans, and referrals to safe houses. Nurse managers may also designate a referral as "mandatory" due to serious work performance problems as part of a Performance Improvement Counseling Plan with consultation from human resources. The EAP counselor assesses the problem and formulates a treatment plan with the client's input. The treatment plan may include a referral to a human resource sponsored workshop, or to a community resource. In cases involving substance abuse or addiction, the nurse must be safe to practice and comply with state licensure requirements and VUMC policy. With monitoring and advocacy from the Nurse Wellness Program of Work/Life Connections-EAP, following treatment, the nurse is able to resume work.

One of the most significant core components of an EAP is the ability to support recovery in the workplace, while maintaining safety compliance protocols of the organization. A self-referred nurse may seek help from the EAP and during the course of the interview disclose symptoms consistent with DSM-IV TR-diagnostic criteria for a substance abuse disorder (American Psychiatric Association, 2000). At that point the EAP has to consider its obligation to two clients: the employee (voluntarily asking for professional help with a problem) and the organization (a medical center having the responsibility to the public for safety). Addiction is a treatable, medical disease. Substance abuse impairs performance. Impaired professionals need treatment. Timely and effective treatment can save a nurse's license, career, and even his or her life. Too often, without this recognition the nurse's license, practice, and the safety of the nurse's patients are jeopardized.

In other cases, the nurse is referred by the organization due to impairment on the job. Should standard of treatment and monitoring requirements differ based on referral status?

The dilemma is how to support the nurse and at the same time ensure public safety. Being licensed is a contract with society. There are some nurses who conceive the process as punitive; however patient safety must trump self-determination. Work/Life Connections-EAP believes that the best chance for achieving and maintaining recovery success for nurses includes the following components:

Competent initial assessment. An independent assessment, conducted by a professional who is external to the organization provides second opinion credibility. Expertise in addictions and occupational psychology is helpful.

Quality treatment. Professionals often need a longer term treatment model to break through the denial and tendency to intellectualize. Treatment is often career and life–saving, not punishment.

Professional advocacy. Professional Nurse advocacy programs sponsored by the state nursing boards are important partners. They may require compliance with some return to work stipulations such as a possible narcotic handling restriction for the first year of sobriety or shift restrictions for the first year with limits on overtime to allow time to attend meetings.

Continuum of care. A formal document outlining the required meetings, screenings, and treatment requirements provides external accountability until the individual internalizes this.

It consists of the following components:

- Return to work agreement with the employer outlining requirements for continued employment (general duration-3 yrs);
- 12-step program participation (AA, NA, peer assistance support groups);
- Random UDS monitoring (professional screening following DOT and SAMI guidelines)
- 1:1 counseling
- Regular EAP (NWP) check-ups (monitoring compliance with recovery support plans)

Consistent messages. Communication between professional advocacy programs, unit managers, and the EAP are imperative to avoid splitting and compliance lapses.

Supportive workplace. The work unit must be receptive to the transition and lifestyle changes that the post treatment nurse is making. This means supporting any restrictions and making attendance at AA meetings possible within schedule constraints.

Workplace Outreach

Trauma support and critical incident stress response services are the chief-outreach components of the Vanderbilt University Nurse Wellness Program. The NWP, in conjunction with Work/Life Connections-EAP, supports staff through workplace traumas such as the death of colleagues, clinical situations involving cases with poor patient outcomes, closure of clinics, reductions in force, patient attacks on staff, multiple deaths on a medical unit, suicide of colleagues, disaster response, and other critical incidents. The issue of dealing with grief and loss significantly impacts a workgroup. Providing a structure and support for responding to the deaths of colleagues and patients can help nurses deal with such stressors.

Nurses and other healthcare workers are at increased risk for being assaulted even though they are providing care and comfort. Having a proactive protocol for workplace response can improve morale, the perception of safety, and the productivity of an entire workgroup (Flannery, 1998). The Nurse Wellness Program of Work/Life Connections-EAP has responded to assaults on nurses. Work/Life Connections-EAP protocol believes an immediate, pro-active and systematic intervention is critical, in order to prevent the assaulted staff member from leaving the organization and the nursing profession entirely. Group interventions with the remaining staff are important to regain a sense of safety and support, allowing staff a forum for dealing with their own critical incident stress resulting from the assault. Concurrently, management must perform procedure critiques of the workplace intervention recording actions taken and ways of preventing recurrence of a similar critical-incident event.

The Nurse Wellness Program and Vanderbilt's Trauma Response CISM Team are both services of Work/Life Connections-EAP. An internal EAP is ideally positioned to provide supportive services in response to traumatic events or critical incidents in the workplace, because it is intimately familiar with the workplace culture. The internal EAP counselor is both a peer (employed by the organization) and a mental health professional. While the International Critical Incident Stress Management model for rescue personnel teaches that Trauma Response Team only responds when called, the EAP model encourages supervisor outreach and pro-active interventions when an incident impacts the workplace (Everly and Mitchell, 1999). Work/Life Connections-EAP has worked with managers to recognize potential needs for a CISM intervention. When a member of the EAP staff becomes aware of a traumatic event, such as an assault or an employee death, which may possibly impact the workplace an informational contact is often made with the supervisor to make available trauma support and critical incident stress response services.

Promoting Wellness

When nurses are struggling with a personal or workplace problem, it is important to address issues of overall preventive wellness issues, as noted above. The NWP works with NWC to focus on improving the emotional health and wellness of VUMC nurses through proactive in-service programs. Some of the most important in-service topics presented by the NWP focus on addressing stress management, balancing work and home, improving communication skills, coping with organizational change, depression, and grief. Providing worksite wellness presentations (i.e., stress resilience, handling loss and grief, encountering distressed patients and their families, etc.) is a method of marketing that builds creditability. The NWP Nurse Champion must work visibly with the existing programs to support services which promote balance and wellness.

EFFECTIVENESS OF THE NWP

As with many mental health interventions, objective outcome data is limited. Self report data collected by the NWP indicates nurses who are seen through the NWP generally report that they feel better and that there is a resolution of their presenting problem. One indicator of the success of the NWP is utilization (the number of nurses opened as EAP clients as well as the number of consultations by managers that were opened separately that concerned specific nurses).

The NWP began September 2002 with the hiring of an EAP Nurse Champion. The 2002-2003, nursing utilization of EAP increased fifty- two percent. By 2003-2004, utilization had climbed to nearly five percent of nurses employed by Vanderbilt University Medical Center with an increase in manager requests for interventions. In 2004-2005, ninety-six percent of the NWP clients were self-referrals with only four percent referred on a mandatory basis, demonstrating acceptance of the NWP by its target population. In 2005-06, there was another 43% increase with a utilization of 198 (representing a penetration of approximately 9-10% of the target population).

Employees who have accessed the Work/Life Connections-EAP, including nurses, have provided the following self-assessment data through an anonymous client satisfaction tool:

- At the time of intake, sixty-five percent of the EAP clients who completed the survey endorsed that "my issues interfered with my work performance."
- After the EAP interventions, eighty-one percent of the EAP clients who completed the survey agreed that "my performance/productivity improved after using Work/Life Connections-EAP."
- Seventy-seven percent of the EAP clients who completed the survey reported "my coping ability improved through contact with Work/Life Connections-EAP."

CONCLUSION

When a university is considering the creation of a specialized program targeting a specific population, certain elements are required. First, there must be a reputable EAP which is utilized and respected that uses program data to regularly assess the needs of the target population. Secondly, there must be a defined need for such a program. Third, the target population must have a grassroots investment in the creation and support of such a program. At Vanderbilt, the conditions were prime for the formation of a specialized NWP. Throughout the entire United States, there is a critical need for hospitals and clinics to focus on the health and wellness needs of nurses. It is important to provide a safe, accessible, confidential workplace sponsored program to intervene when stress, depression, loss, addictions, childcare, eldercare, and relationships interfere with the health and well being of the nurse. The employee assistance model includes the core components needed to provide a successful service. The nurses, who are the target population, must accept the program as credible, confidential, fair, and safe. Based upon the experience at Vanderbilt, adding the component of a nurse EAP counselor to "champion" the program is critical for the success of the program. This champion must be active, visible, and respected by the nursing staff, managers, and administration. A healthy balance between work and home is critical for retaining quality nurses and attracting quality candidates into the profession. The demands on nurses will only increase, while the current labor force will continue to age and decrease in size. It is crucial for the nurse to take care of herself/himself, in order to avoid burnout thus retaining the seasoned, skilled nurse in the profession. Specialized-program initiatives serving nurses must be approached as ongoing efforts, not just one time "quick fixes." Wellness is a process, not an event. Healthy work environments that treat employees as valuable resources will find greater success in recruitment and retention efforts. Nurses at Vanderbilt University have embraced the NWP and benefit from its services.

ACKNOWLEDGMENTS

Mary Yarbrough, MD, MPH, Director of Health and Wellness and Work/Life Connections-EAP; Marilyn Dubree, MSN, RN, Chief Nursing Officer; Adrienne Ames, MSN, RN, the Nurses at Vanderbilt University Medical Center, the Work/Life Connections-EAP staff and Vanderbilt University Medical Center leadership.

REFERENCES

Aiken, L. H., Clarke, S. P., Sloane, D. M., Sochalski, J., & Silber, J. H. (2002) Hospital nurse staffing and patient mortality, nurse burnout and job dissatisfaction [Electronic version]. *JAMA*. *288*(16), 1987-1993.

American Psychiatric Association. (2000). *Diagnostic and statistical manual of mental disorders, (4th ed., TR.)* Washington, DC: Author.

Bratt, M. M., Broome, M., Kelber, S. & Lostocco, L. (2000). Influence of stress and nursing leadership on job satisfaction of pediatric intensive care unit nurses [Electronic version]. *American Journal of Critical Care. 9*(5), 307-317.

Buerhaus, P., Donelan, K., Ulrich, B., Norman, L., & Dittus, R. (2006).State of the Registered Nurse Workforce in the United States [Electronic version]. *Nurse Econ. 24*(1), 6-12.

Buerhaus, P. & Needleman, J. (2000). Policy implication of research on nurse staffing and quality of care [Electronic version]. *Policy, Politics & Nursing Practice. 1*(1), 5-16.

Cottrell, S. (2000). Occupational Stress and Job Satisfaction in Mental Health Nursing: Focused Interventions via Evidence-based Assessment [Electronic version]. *The Journal of Psychiatric and Mental Health Nursing.*

Davey, E., (2000, October 16). *Nurses face suicide risk.* Retrieved April25, 2006, from http://www.cix.co.uk/~ldsk/news63.htm.

Everly, G. .S., Jr, and Mitchell, J. T. (1999) *Critical incident stress management (CISM): a new era and standard in crisis intervention* (2nd ed.). Ellicott City, MD: Chevron Publishing Corporation.

Feskanich, D., Hastrup, J.L.,Marshall,J.R.,Colditz, G.A.,Stampler, W.J., Willett,W.C. and Kawachi,I.(2002.). Stress and Suicide in the Nurses' Health Study [Electronic version]. *Journal of Epidemiological Community Health.* 56;95-98.

Flannery, R.B., Jr. (1998) *The Assaulted Staff Action Program (ASAP): Coping with the psychological aftermath of violenc.* Ellicott City, MD: Chevron Publishing Corporation.

Foxall, M. J., Zimmerman, L., Standley, R., & Bene, B. (1990). A comparison of frequency and sources of nursing job stress perceived by intensive care, hospice and medical-surgical nurses [Electronic version]. *Journal of Advanced Nursing. 15*(5), 577-84.

MedHunters Staff. (2004, November). Depression and Nursing. *MedHunters.com.* Retrieved April 25, 2006, from http://www.medhunters.com/articles/depression And Nursing.html.

O'Neil, E. & Seago, J.A. (2002). Editorial: Meeting the challenge of nursing and the nation's health [Electronic version]. *JAMA. 288*, 2040-2041.

Rogers, A. E., Hwang, W.T., & Scott, L.D. (2004). The effects of work breaks on staff nurse performance [Electronic version]. *Journal of Nursing Administration, 34*(11), 512-519.

Tennessee Professional Assistance Program. (2004). Retrieved April 25, 2006, from http://www.tnpap.org/about.html.

VUMC works to retain quality nurses: Dubree. (2002, May 10). *The Reporter.* Retrieved April 25, 2006, from http://www.mc.vanderbilt.edu/reporter/index.html ?ID=2098.

doi:10.1300/J490v22n03_08

A Manager Coaching Group Model: Applying Leadership Knowledge

Monica Scamardo
Susan C. Harnden

SUMMARY. This article describes a model, benefits, and outcomes of a coaching and support group for managers. Professionals in the University of Texas at Austin Employee Assistance Program have created manager groups to support and coach managers in areas of skill development, including interpersonal challenges and communication, while providing a confidential forum for professional discussion. It is basic practice for EAPs to provide support to employees dealing with personal problems and one-on-one consultation for managers about an employee; however, few, if any, EAPs provide group coaching for managers in their roles as leaders. By facilitating manager groups EAPs can help reduce managers' stress and build their supportive and professional networks while helping to develop managers' communication and "soft skills." A model is presented to demonstrate the format of the manager groups facilitated at the University of Texas at Austin. doi:10.1300/J490v22n03_09 *[Article copies available for a fee from The Haworth Document Delivery Service: 1-800-HAWORTH. E-mail address: <docdelivery@haworthpress.com> Website: <http://www.HaworthPress.com> © 2006/2007 by The Haworth Press, Inc. All rights reserved.]*

KEYWORDS. Managers, leadership, coaching, Employee Assistance Program, support, skill development, soft skills

[Haworth co-indexing entry note]: "A Manager Coaching Group Model: Applying Leadership Knowledge." Scamardo, Monica, and Susan C. Harnden. Co-published simultaneously in *Journal of Workplace Behavioral Health* (The Haworth Press, Inc.) Vol. 22, No. 2/3, 2006/2007, pp. 127-143; and: *Employee Assistance Programs in Higher Education* (ed: R. Paul Maiden and Sally B. Philips) The Haworth Press, 2006/2007, pp. 127-143. Single or multiple copies of this article are available for a fee from The Haworth Document Delivery Service [1-800-HAWORTH, 9:00 a.m. - 5:00 p.m. (EST). E-mail address: docdelivery@haworthpress.com].

Available online at http://jwbh.haworthpress.com

doi:10.1300/J490v22n03_09

INTRODUCTION

Employee Assistance Professionals provide services that promote the mental, emotional, and physical well-being of employees. Personal counseling and referral services, offered by Employee Assistance Programs (EAP), support employees during difficult times when dealing with such issues as anxiety, depression, grief, loss, relationship problems and substance abuse. Manager consulting services offered by EAPs most commonly support and coach the leaders of the organization through challenging situations with employees. It is common for EAPs to offer counseling groups, yet, few, if any, offer groups for managers who are dealing with common challenges like workgroup dynamics or interpersonal communication challenges, both of which call for the use of relational or "soft skills."

These are the types of skills that much of the research reports is crucial for managers to develop into successful leaders. Goleman (1997) suggests that technical skills and knowledge that make one qualified for a job but that it is one's interpersonal ability that makes one successful on the job. Much of the leadership research supports the idea of developing these types of abilities, often called "soft skills" (Fleenor, 2003; Goleman 2002; Kornik, 2006; Lombardo & Eichinger 2001). But how does one develop or apply the knowledge of interpersonal or "soft skills" they may have read in a book or heard in a training? The model in this article outlines a group for managers who are focused on further developing leadership skills that include "soft skill" abilities.

MANAGERS AS LEADERS: DEVELOPING "SOFT SKILLS"

Managers face many challenges related to the businesses they are in as well as with the people they manage and lead. So how does one become a manager who gets the work accomplished and leads so that teams are inspired to follow and succeed? Developing leaders is seen as the greatest challenge for 2006 according to The Ken Blanchard Companies (Kornik, 2006).

A significant and challenging part of a manager's role is utilizing what are called "soft skills," interpersonal skills or relational skills. Dr. John Fleenor of the Center for Creative Leadership says that "soft skills," such as establishing trust, displaying empathy and communicating effectively make all the difference in leading others (April 2003). Weaknesses in "soft skills" prevent leaders from effectively managing change. A recent survey conducted by The Center suggests that the greater the stress in the organization, the more important the leader's "soft skills" become. Managers in this survey reported some of their greatest challenges to be motivating staff, communicating clearly, and developing staff.

In the 2005 Changing Nature of Leadership report, the skills most important for future leaders and managers were building relationships, collaboration and change management, all of which are "soft skills." A well-known leadership development program by Lombardo and Eichinger (2001) outlines managerial competencies that are most related to performance. Many of the competencies they find in effective managers are interpersonal skills (i.e., conflict management, trust, motivating others).

Similarly, Daniel Goleman, author of *Primal Leadership* (2002), discusses four competency areas that are tied to effective and successful leaders' interpersonal skills. The fourth competency area in particular is called "relationship management." Within this competency Goleman discusses the importance of conflict management, teamwork, and collaboration.

There are hundreds of leadership development programs and workshops offered every year that provide research and didactic information to managers developing their leadership styles. Interestingly, in a study by Novations Group, 34% of respondents told researchers that their leadership development programs needed updating and improvement (Pomeroy, 2006). Many training programs provide the information but may fall short in the areas of application, coaching, support, and actual skill development.

What Is Coaching?

Coaching emerged as a field with a central function to facilitate personal and/or professional change and development (Hudson, 1999). By the late 1980's corporate coaching emerged with a purpose to impact both individuals and organizations by promoting continuous resilience and performance. Coaching is currently being positioned as an employee work/life benefit for high-potential, high-performing employees, according to an article by Ann Vincola featured with HR.com in 2003.

Coaches function as generalists who draw from their vast experiences to motivate, facilitate and guide their clients toward positive change (Hudson, 1999). Coaches connect short-term strategies to long-term goals. Coaches are change agents who look at things from different perspectives, take risks, inspire others to be their best, are future-oriented, confront destructive behaviors, provide support during times of transition, are good communicators, and facilitate learning, training and referrals. Stern (2004) discusses several situations in which coaching can be especially effective for leaders' development: conveying specific performance expectations, techniques for giving direct feedback, building organizational values and strategy, shaping constructive conflict management techniques, and building comfort with ambiguity.

Hudson (1999) defines one-on-one, group coaching, and systems coaching. One-on-one coaching is working with individual clients in one- to two-hour sessions over an agreed upon length of time. These meetings are focused on how the individual can be more effective as a human being and as a professional. Group coaching is conducted with several clients who have a shared interest. Developing effective communication and leadership development are examples of common interests of those in an organizational coaching group. Systems coaching refers to working with a system (i.e., organization, government agency, workgroup) to enhance visionary planning, morale, and renewal of purpose. It is believed that by working with key people and departments that this type of coaching promotes alignment with the system's mission.

In 2003 CompassPoint Nonprofit Services conducted a yearlong study called The Executive Coaching Project. This project underscored "the need to develop various strategies for supporting and retaining leadership talent in the nonprofit sector." The results of the study showed the positive impact of coaching managers including: increased task completion and productivity, improved personnel management skills, and improved communication with staff.

USEFULNESS AND EFFECTIVENESS OF SUPPORT GROUPS

Group therapy was first introduced in the 1940's and has since taken on multiple forms, including support groups (Yalom, 1995). Support groups provide a discussion forum for members who have identified shared challenges. The members come together to provide each other with various types of nonprofessional help through the sharing of resources, information, and support. Group therapy, led by a professional, provides a psychotherapeutic process shared between people who have experienced similar problems resulting in psychological distress or interpersonal issues.

Irvin Yalom, MD is known for his research on and practice of group work. Much of what he writes outlines the usefulness and effectiveness of groups. Although the groups themselves are different, people find psychotherapy and support groups beneficial for similar reasons. The common factors are: the instillation of hope, universality, imparting information, altruism, and imitative behavior (Yalom, 1995).

Instillation of Hope

The instillation and maintenance of hope is an important part of the group experience for most members. It facilitates motivation toward making changes and developing new skills during the most challenging of times. Hearing the stories of others who are in different stages of the same problem can reassure members that they too will manage.

Universality

Many people feel they are alone because of the uniqueness of their situation or the amount of interference the problem is causing in their usual ability to function. Through support groups the universality of such challenges are discussed and failures and successes are shared. The feeling of inadequacy or incompetence is common when attempting to manage a problem yet it is through interacting and the support from others that members can overcome these uncertainties.

Imparting Information

Throughout the group attendance members gain information that they did not have previously. Information may be provided didactically through educating or through direct advice from the members. The purpose of imparting didactic instruction is to transfer information, alter patterns, and structure the group. The most effective advice from group members is reported to be systematic instructions or alternative suggestions about how to achieve a goal (Piper, McCallum, & Azim, 1992).

Altruism

People receive through the act of giving. Group members are extremely helpful to each other because of what they "give." They offer support, reassurance, suggestions and insight. Altruism plays a significant role in the success of support groups and creates interpersonal connections between the members.

Imitating Behavior

Much of what we learn is through observing and imitating behavior. In support groups members can benefit through "imitating" what has worked for others. Imitative behavior allows members to experiment with possible solutions and possibly avoid what others have tried that has not worked.

EMPLOYEE ASSISTANCE PROGRAMS

Employee Assistance Programs (EAP) provide a variety of services to employees. Many factors determine the scope and focus of EAP services. The nature of the industry or business in which they reside, the presence of unions, and external or internal status are among a few of the influences. There are a set of core functions that are common to all EAPs. Employee Assistance Professionals Association (EAPA) describes these core technology functions. Several apply directly to services provided for managers:

1. Consultation with, training of, and assistance to work organization leadership (managers, supervisors, and union stewards) seeking to manage the troubled employee, enhance the work environment, and improve employee job performance.
2. Confidential and timely problem identification/assessment for employee clients with personal concerns that may affect job performance.
3. Use of constructive confrontation, motivation, and short-term intervention with employee clients to address problems that affect job performance.
4. Identification of the effects of EAP services on the work organization and individual job performance.

To provide services in the core technology areas EAPs offer programs such as: wellness promotion, work/life, conflict management, violence prevention/threat assessment teams, critical incident/stress management, individual assessment and referral, and manager consultation. An informal benchmarking survey of higher education EAPs completed by the UT EAP in 2005 indicated that current services offered to managers are primarily related to consultation on managing troubled employees and conflict resolution. Such EAPs also reported offering training focused on improving communication, conflict resolution, stress management, and creating positive work environments. None of the EAPs surveyed at the time of this paper reported offering manager support or coaching groups.

THE UNIVERSITY OF TEXAS AT AUSTIN EMPLOYEE ASSISTANCE PROGRAM

The University of Texas at Austin (UT) has 19,000 employees and approximately 360 different departments. Almost 3000 of those employees are managers. In addition there are 17 deans and almost 100 chairs who also manage both faculty and staff.

The UT EAP is internal and uniquely positioned to serve the varied needs of employees. Services are offered and developed as a response to the specific needs of the UT community and are protected by state confidentiality laws that provide a safe environment for employees to explore concerns, options and challenges. The EAP provides short-term individual counseling and referral, training, and manager consultation. When requested by employees, the EAP can collaborate with other Human Resource Services to provide comprehensive and collaborative consultation.

How Do Employees Become Managers?

Throughout years of consulting with managers on their career goals and preparation for leadership positions, the authors estimate that half of the managers they have worked with have reported that they never actually intended to become managers but have done so for a variety of reasons. Many said they became managers because of the quality of their work, as a reward for their performance. It is assumed managers have expertise in their departments or organizations, however, it is unclear how prepared they are to lead and how skilled they are at communicating, negotiating, motivating, or building trust and morale. As discussed earlier the literature suggests that the development of "soft skills" determines the success of a leader. What venues are available to managers to transform their skills into leadership?

At UT Austin a manager's initial foundational training is laid out in a three day workshop called Managing @ UT. This program provides an overview of employment law, human resources policies and procedures, and best practices in management. Participants learn how to apply this knowledge and improve their competencies through interactive exercises, group activities, case studies, and self-assessments. Presentations are provided by representatives from Human Resource Services (HRS) including: Recruiting and Staffing, Compensation, Leave Management, Employee Opportunity Services, Employee Relations, Benefits, Worker's Compensation, Compliance, Health and Safety, Records and Employee Assistance.

In addition, managers have access to consultation with these HRS departments and Training Services on teambuilding, performance management, compensation, leave management, worker's compensation, health and safety, and hiring and retention. Individual manager coaching and consultation, threat assessment, fitness for duty, and critical incident stress management are some of the additional services offered at no cost, as part of employees' benefits packages, through the UT EAP. Common reasons managers consult with the UT EAP include: dealing with job stress and organizational change, skill development, concerns about employee behavior, challenges with employee performance, team dynamics, difficulties with their own managers, goal setting, and strategies for effective communication.

Even with these resources there are many gaps in facilitating the professional growth of managers as leaders. How do managers transform the skills they learn in trainings and consultation and develop them into practical and creative abilities that their teams are inspired to follow? Managers tell us they are missing ongoing discussions with other managers about how to apply the skills they have learned and adapt the skills they have when challenged by difficult and complex problems. It is this gap the manager group strives to fill.

DEVELOPING THE MANAGER GROUP

Preparation

After several years of consulting with UT managers and hearing their challenges, the authors of this article decided to gather a group of managers together to discuss the idea of a manager group. A focus group was developed to identify the topics and format that would be most beneficial to managers. The 16 members of the focus group were those who had attended previous manager trainings conducted by the EAP professionals. The managers affirmed what was suspected. While they believed there is a place for didactic learning, they stated the need for a time and a place to discuss what they already knew as well as the challenges of applying these skills in difficult situations. In addition, the managers said they wanted to hear from other managers to help them understand the realities of the environment they work in and to decrease their sense of isolation. The topics they identified as useful for discussion included: team-building tools and techniques; managing for outcomes; communication and conflict management skills; and setting, communicating and following through on realistic expectations.

Not only did they want a place to discuss problems and concerns and get feedback on these topics, they wanted much of the focus to be on creative problem solving and honing their soft skills. Logistically, the managers suggested meetings every other week during the lunch hour to accommodate demanding work schedules.

The Groups

Four separate manager support groups have been facilitated since March 2005 and the fifth and sixth groups will occur in Fall 2006. The number of managers who have committed to each of the five groups has ranged between five and seventeen members. The managers represent various departments from academia and research as well as accounting, technology, computer services, libraries, physical plant, and development. The managers have a range of experience. Some of the managers are new while others have 15 years of experience or more. The managers in the groups thus far have supervised 2 to 35 employees. Up to this point, three of the participants have been male and 44 have been female.

The group is advertised via university-wide emails as well as being promoted during other EAP trainings and presentations. The group is also listed on the EAP calendar of events webpage and other HRS departments have recommended it to participants. Members self-select to attend and enrollment is open to any manager who is interested in attending.

Prior to the initial group meeting the facilitators email those registered to gather information about experience levels, number of employees supervised, and to gain an understanding of the interest in the group. The managers report various reasons they are interested in joining the group:

- "I signed up for this group because I want to enhance my skills as a manager. . . . I'd like to be a more intentional manager."
- ". . . to better understand the UT perspective on management and learn from others on how to handle issues that come up."

- "I would like to address the problem of gaining respect from the ones I supervise since I was a co-worker in their group when I was first hired at UT."
- "I need to talk to people outside my area about problems."
- "I need support. This is a hard job!"
- "I realize how important it is to delegate (even complicated things) rather than do things myself so that others learn and are better prepared to take over when I retire."
- "So I can meet other managers around campus and collaborate on solutions."

The Manager Group Model

The initial group meeting is mandatory and begins with introductions of the members and facilitator, and an overview of the structure of the group, including the importance of confidentiality. Also unique to the initial meeting is the goal-setting workshop. This is based on the authors' beliefs that well defined goals improve the performance of managers and employees alike but that often goals are developed in such a way to render them ineffective as a tool to promote positive change. In this meeting managers are trained to use the SMARTER format to set goals (specific, measurable, attainable, realistic, timelines, evaluate, and redo). Each manager creates an individual, manager goal that will foster professional development and that is aligned with the mission of their department. After setting their goal the managers then develop anchors that are descriptors on each end of a Likert-type scale to measure the progress toward the goal. One end of the scale constitutes "no progress" toward the goal while the other end of the scale represents "full goal attainment." Using this tool the managers can track their efforts and report on their progress to the rest of group.

Each group meeting is an hour and fifteen minutes. For each subsequent meeting a topic is designated from the list generated by the focus group or other topics of interest suggested by a current member. Topics include:

- Communicating Expectations
- Initiating Difficult Conversations
- Negotiating with employees, peers and directors
- Building Trust and Morale
- Motivating Employees

- Effective Decision Making
- Managing the Impact of Change

The managers are asked to come prepared each week with an example of a challenge and a success in the topic area. This ensures a rich group discussion. As each manager discusses their challenge, other managers are encouraged to share possible solutions drawing on the situations in which they had been successful. Depending on the topic, role-play simulations, mini-presentations, and resources are included in the meetings. Lastly, managers report on the progress they are making toward the goals they set in the first meeting or they discuss alterations they have made to the actual goal (i.e., timelines, measurements).

Manager Experiences and Outcomes of the Group

Managers in these groups share problems and learn from other's experiences with similar challenges. For example:

- **Managers receive practical feedback on negotiating with directors.** One manager wanted to provide corrective action to an employee but believed the director of the program would not support her and wanted suggestions for how to get the director to "buy-in." Other managers in the group provided her with feedback about similar situations in which they negotiated with their directors. One manager said he explained to his manager that the corrective action was necessary in order to maintain the morale among the team and to accomplish the goals of the department. Another described to her manager the financial cost to the organization. Each of these two managers described how, over time, they gained support from their directors which encouraged the other manager to do the same.
- **Managers receive information about resources that they were not previously aware of.** Some of the managers were not aware that they could receive consultation from HRS representatives about performance management, teambuilding, and evaluations which are tailored to their unique situation.
- **Managers receive feedback on change management.** A new manager was challenged by the need to implement new technology in order to provide the services demanded. She believed her employees to be resistant to any type of change. Most of them had worked in the department for more than 10 years and they had not

integrated the use of technology as basic as voicemail. She received feedback from the facilitator and other managers on realistic timeframes, ways to communicate expectations, and the need for additional training for some of her employees.

- **Managers discuss solutions that the group maybe familiar with but are having difficulty putting into action.** A manager discussed having a difficult interaction with an employee whose communication style instigated conflict. The manager described how she spoke to this employee and the results of addressing the conflict directly. This encouraged other managers to take action. The facilitator discussed specific strategies and the group role–played scenarios that illustrated approaches and responses so the managers were prepared for a variety of results.
- **Managers talk about how they feel about giving their employees negative feedback.** One manager said she had a great deal of difficulty tolerating people being angry with her and discussed how this caused her to avoid being direct. The facilitators and group members shared similar and different reactions which lead to interesting discussions on communications styles in the workplace.
- **Managers discussed the challenges of motivating employees and specifically motivating employees working in a large state institution.** They shared ideas about recognition as well as systemic changes that allowed for employees to be more in control of their work and make more direct connections between their work and the services provided to customers.

The managers in the groups are frequently given feedback by the facilitator and by the other members about realistic expectations, timeframes, and communication techniques. This enables them to see that attempts to problem solve have potential they have not previously seen and they are then able to sustain their efforts. When they have difficulty envisioning alternatives they role-play scenarios and receive additional feedback.

Throughout the series managers report on the progress related to the goals they established at the beginning of the series and receive feedback about making the goals more focused and effective. Managers from the completed groups said they benefited from the accountability provided through the discussion. Some managers change their goals as a result of feedback. Examples of goal accomplishments are:

- Defined job descriptions with staff input and put specific information about job tasks into a relational database.
- Increased ability and effectiveness at delegation by breaking tasks down into smaller parts then identifying areas in which staff needed further training and communicated action plan to staff.
- Reviewed job descriptions and ways that staff collaborated on specific projects. Through this the manager identified a need for greater clarity about job responsibilities. As a result of this process she also identified a questionable position and consulted with HRS who determined the position should be eliminated in order to reallocate resources toward more appropriate positions.
- Worked toward getting diverse groups to work more effectively together while rewriting a website. This improved visibility, supported greater collaboration, and created more appreciation among team members.
- Developed a schedule of staff meetings and created specific duties and responsibilities of everyone attending.
- Reorganized structure for staff meetings and added an agenda that improved productivity and communication.

At the final group meeting surveys are distributed to the members made up of Likert scales and short answer questions. In one section managers were asked, "How did the group contribute to you making progress toward your goals?" Some of the responses included:

- . . . by getting organized it was easier to forecast the departmental needs."
- "Putting it in writing helped me see the purpose of the meetings and communicate about them more effectively."
- "(The group) caused me to pay attention to this goal on an ongoing basis."
- "The group heightened my attention to my goal."
- "It was a better use of resources."

Group Benefits

The group, although not a psychotherapeutic process, fulfills common factors shown to be beneficial in group therapy: the instillation of hope, universality, imparting information, altruism, and imitative behavior.

Instillation of hope. As a result of the group managers have reported that they felt better able to manage effectively and more confident in their abilities to set and reach their professional goals. They also said it gave them confidence in their ability to manage change more successfully.

Universality. Managers from the focus group and in the support group said that they previously felt isolated. As the managers begin to share their experiences with employees and the complex processes needed to manage, many have come to recognize the concerns they have in common and have therefore developed more realistic expectations.

Imparting Information. When discussing topics such as building trust and morale and motivating employees, managers shared specific strategies that have worked for them. Members of the groups shared creative ideas that ranged from specific ways to motivate individual employees to general approaches that communicated respect and inspired employees to contribute more fully.

Altruism. Managers expressed pride in their ability to offer ideas to other managers and said they felt rewarded by making this contribution. Managers with more experience enthusiastically offered suggestions and recommendations based on their previous experiences. Outside of the group meeting one set of managers corresponded regularly on an employee issue which reportedly benefited both of them and the employee's performance improved. Another manager group continued to meet after the formal group ended to continue to support each other and discuss important managerial issues over a longer period of time.

Imitative. Managers offered specific examples of ways to communicate with employees and to set goals that improved work processes. As a response other managers attempted to communicate in similar ways and developed goals based on the successes of other managers' experiences and successes.

LESSONS LEARNED AND FUTURE DIRECTIONS

As it stands the past group participants report that the current model offers a good forum to discuss challenges and develop additional skills that enhance managerial leadership. The past group participants have also referred colleagues to the group. The managers say they have learned to implement strategies that are positively related to how they communicate with their teams and their own managers. They report feeling more confident in their abilities and their managerial decisions.

The authors, who are the facilitators of the groups, have also learned some valuable information during their experience creating and conducting the groups:

- Groups need to be offered consistently and predictably to build an expectation as a reliable resource and to respond to referrals from current managers. Manager groups at UT will be offered at least once each academic semester.
- Experienced managers benefit most from a forum that allows them to discuss training received, expertise, application of principles, and creative adaptation in challenging situations. The current model discussed in this article meets the needs of middle managers. The authors and facilitators of the current group will continue to offer the group and utilize feedback from members over time so that the group evolves with the needs of the members.
- Managers are invested in supporting a peer facilitated group at the end of the series. The facilitator of the manager group will encourage any members interested in continuing the connection with other members by distributing a list of the contact information of those interested.
- Managers often have difficulty reaching goals they have set for themselves because the goals are not focused on behaviors and skills the manager has control over, the goals are overly vague, have unrealistic time frames, or are abandoned when not being met rather than being rewritten. Ongoing education about goal setting and achievement as well as change management will continue to be an integral part of the manager group model.
- An ideal group size for this model is 10 participants or less. This allows enough time for all members to contribute to the group discussions as well as establishing relationships and networking between members.
- This concept and model may be limited based on organizational size and environment.

At this point in the creation of the manager group model the authors are setting their own goals related to the future direction and evolution of the group.

- The current name of the group, *Manager Support Group*, is being changed to *Manager Coaching Group* to better reflect the current process and purpose of the group.
- We are considering expanding the number of sessions in the group model: an initial session for goal setting and eight to ten follow up sessions for topics and goal check-in. This would allow for additional topics to be discussed, more time to focus on the progress of

individual goal achievement, and to further strengthen the cohesiveness between the group members, facilitating, ongoing, informal meetings for the future of the members. Meeting every other week rather than every week is also being considered.
- The facilitators have been invited into a department to run the group for the department's managers. The process and outcome of this "internal" manager group may provide additional information on an altered model to be used with such groups.
- The needs of new managers should be addressed in groups that incorporate a significant amount of time in didactic learning and structure. Therefore, a group for new managers is being designed to meet the unique needs of this managerial level.
- The authors plan to research ways in which the impact of the group can be quantitatively measured or qualitatively analyzed.

As EAP professionals we are in the position to positively impact the health and effectiveness of an organization as well as the mental, emotional and physical well being of the individual employees. One of the most influential ways this is done is to effect the environment by positively influencing the leadership of the organization. Managers at all levels have influence over morale, effective communication, and motivation and yet, due to lack of information, skills, training or knowledge gaps, managers may, at best, not take full advantage of their ability to influence the work environment and at worst may damage it. As EAP professionals we can assist and influence this process by intervening effectively with managers. A manager's ability to lead effectively has far reaching effects. Those who manage set the tone for the environment, impact the focus and direction of the organization, and can inspire others to excel professionally. This manager group model allows EAP professionals to multiply their efforts by using the strengths of managers to motivate them to excel as leaders.

ACKNOWLEDGMENTS

The authors would like to thank the members of the focus group and the members of the manager groups for their interest and feedback regarding the development and evolution of the group model as well as for sharing their management experiences.

We would also like to thank the members of the UT EAP staff for collaborating with us on the vision of the group, supporting its occurrence, and for their editorial feedback on this manuscript. Thank you to Connie Deutsch, Rita Handrich, Melinda Robillard, and Jeff Stellmach.

REFERENCES

Creative leadership, tough times: Soft skills make the difference (2003). *President & CEO*, 36-37.

Goleman, D., Boyatzis, R., & McKee A. (2002). Primal leadership: Realizing the power of emotional intelligence. Boston, MA: Harvard Business School Press.

Goleman, D. (1995). Emotional intelligence. New York, NY: Bantam.

Hudson, F. M. (1999). Handbook of coaching. San Francisco: Jossey-Bass Publishers.

Kornik, J. (2006). On the minds of managers . . . skills shortages and new leadership. *Training, 43*(6), 16-16.

Lombardo, M. M. & Eichinger, R. W. (2001). The leadership machine. Lominger Limited Inc.

Martin, Andre (2005). The changing nature of leadership (The Center for Creative Leadership). Greensboro, NC: Online Publication.

Pomeroy, A. (2006). Train leaders with corporate strategy in mind. HR Magazine, *51*(6), 24.

Stern, L. R. (2004). Executive coaching: A working definition. *Consulting Psychology Journal: Practice and Research, 56*(3), 154-162.

Vincola, A. (2003). Executive coaching . . . not just for executives anymore. HR.com, August 2003.

doi:10.1300/J490v22n03_09

University of Arizona Life and Work Connections: A Synergistic Strategy for Maximizing Whole-Person Productivity over the Employees' Life-Cycle/Work-Cycle

Darci A. Thompson
David L. Swihart

SUMMARY. The concept of integration has emerged in recent years as a strategy considered by providers of employee assistance, wellness and work-life services to meet the changing needs of the organizations they serve. There continues to be much discussion, however, about what exactly integration is, and how to do it. Beginning with a definition of integration, this article seeks to contribute to the discussion by describing the University of Arizona (UA) Life and Work Connections, a program that was conceived from its development to be an integrated service model. The theoretical and philosophical backgrounds of the program are presented and translated into the UA Life and Work Connections model. Advantages of the model and challenges to integration are discussed, and a detailed case study of a critical incident response is presented. doi:10.1300/J490v22n03_10 *[Article copies available for a fee from The Haworth Document Delivery Service: 1-800-HAWORTH. E-mail address:*

[Haworth co-indexing entry note]: "University of Arizona Life and Work Connections: A Synergistic Strategy for Maximizing Whole-Person Productivity over the Employees' Life-Cycle/Work-Cycle." Thompson, Darci A., and David L. Swihart. Co-published simultaneously in *Journal of Workplace Behavioral Health* (The Haworth Press, Inc.) Vol. 22, No. 2/3, 2006/2007, pp. 145-160; and: *Employee Assistance Programs in Higher Education* (ed: R. Paul Maiden and Sally B. Philips) The Haworth Press, 2006/2007, pp. 145-160. Single or multiple copies of this article are available for a fee from The Haworth Document Delivery Service [1-800-HAWORTH, 9:00 a.m. - 5:00 p.m. (EST). E-mail address: docdelivery@haworthpress.com].

Available online at http://jwbh.haworthpress.com

doi:10.1300/J490v22n03_10

KEYWORDS. Integration, health and productivity management, employee assistance, EAP, work-life, wellness, academe, domains, life-cycle, work-cycle, whole-person

INTRODUCTION

Integrating employee assistance, work-life, and wellness programs has become one of the dominant topics of discussion among EAPs at the present time. At issue are three questions: What is integration; how does it work; and will it really offer employers more robust services that enhance employee health and productivity? *UA Life & Work Connections*, on the campus of the University of Arizona, has had a unique opportunity to create an integrated program from inception over the past 14 years. Exploring ways the program developed and is operated provides one example of how these key questions are answered.

The University of Arizona (UA), located in Tucson, is a major academic research institution with a large health sciences campus and teaching hospital. As of fiscal year 2003 to 2004, the UA has 37,000 students and nearly 11,500 FTE employees. The UA has a number of world-renowned research and academic departments, including Astronomy, the Lunar and Planetary Laboratory, Optics and Medicine. The 2004 fiscal year total revenue was slightly over $1 billion, of which nearly $400 million came in the form of research grants and contracts (University of Arizona Office of Decision Planning and Support, 2004).

UA Life & Work Connections was created in 1990 and developed as the result of remarkable foresight on the part of many university employees. Originally associated with the campus health service as "Employee Wellness," it soon became part of the human resources department when an employee assistance feature was added. Over the next ten years, child care, elder care, and work-life support components were added and the program became known as UA Life & Work Connections (LWC).

Remarkably, LWC's creators recognized the value of building an "integrated" program. Long before it was the subject of much discussion, integration was envisioned as a means to carry out LWC's strategic plan. Since its inception, the program's plan has been to provide, within the domains of worksite wellness, employee assistance, and work-life support, as many services as are feasible (without sacrificing quality) to as many employees as possible, while maximizing available resources. The risk was that the program was a sink or swim proposition; fortunately, LWC swam well.

Starting in 1999, the LWC staff team began meeting to document LWC's operational model and to articulate their concept of integration. This process led to the following definition of integration as used by LWC:

> Integration: Bringing together, in a synergistic way, the specialized knowledge and trained expertise of professionals in different but related fields in order to better serve the organization and its employees. (Swihart & Thompson, 2002)

PHILOSOPHY BEHIND LWC'S INTEGRATION

Five concepts are incorporated within LWC's definition of integration: *Systems Theory, whole-person, synergy, differentiation and resiliency and life-cycle/work-cycle.*

Systems Theory

Systems theory examines interactions between an individual and his systemic environment. Its application within LWC's model is to identify interactions between an employee and his environment that negatively affect the individual's productivity. Multiple environmental systems are involved within the general realms of work and family.

One systems theory application to the health field is called the "social ecology of health" (Grzywacz & Fuqua, 1999). This theory describes how to maximize the effect of health resources by focusing them on four "leverage points" (socioeconomic status, family, work, and school), so named because of their disproportionate influence on individual health (Grzywacz & Fuqua, 1999; Grzywacz, 2000; Grzywacz & Marks, 2000). By focusing resources on these leverage points, this disproportionate influence becomes an advantage by multiplying the power of the resources. The social ecology of health perspective places equal focus on both the person and the environment as influencing factors on health. Certain qualities of an individual influence his health, while his environment influences health as "a set of nested, interacting systems"

(Grzywacz & Fuqua, 1999). Environmental systems commonly consist of partner relationships, children, extended family, networks of friends, churches (examples associated with the family leverage point); immediate work culture, supervisor and co-worker relationships, and the broader work environment (work leverage point).

Some of these "nested, interacting systems" became evident in 2004 when half of the United States' anticipated influenza vaccine turned out to be tainted and unusable. The ensuing reactions reverberated from the international level down to the individual level as elderly people across the country scrambled to get vaccinated before the supplies were exhausted.

The vaccine disruption is also a good example of a systemic phenomenon called spillover. Spillover occurs when events or conditions in one system cannot be contained, and thus, affect other systems. When news of the vaccine shortage broke, individuals became worried and stressed. From one system to the next, the effects "spilled over," disrupting people, agencies, and institutions.

Individual factors are on the other side of the health influence equation. The social ecology of health asserts that a person's disposition, resources, and characteristics are mediating factors in health (Grzywacz & Fuqua, 1999). Self-care habits, physiology, emotional traits, priorities, self-image, thought patterns, genetic makeup, social skills, and their mutual interactions differ from person to person, leading to idiosyncratic influences on personal health. Consequently, the form and degree of spillover will also be unique, and so intervention efforts must then also fit the individual.

The social ecology of health model applies systems theory to public health issues in a general population; LWC has applied this same framework to productivity issues in the workplace. In the former case, spillover affects health and population-wide epidemiology. In the LWC case, spillover diminishes an employee's performance, affecting the overall performance in the workplace. In this context, the same two leverage points are relevant: family and work. It should be noted here that, technically, spillover can be a positive force also. In the context of this article, spillover specifically refers to negative spillover.

When spillover occurs, the disruption that carries over from one system to another is transmitted through the employee, and can be thought of as waves that pass through the person. Many "domains" of life can therefore be affected when this happens: emotions, thoughts, psychological health, physical health, spirituality, relationships, etc. So when spillover prompts an employee to seek assistance, the most comprehensive approach is to provide assistance from a "whole-person" perspective.

Whole-Person

Having a whole-person view of human beings is the primary driving force behind an integrated service format. In the real world, nobody can completely lay aside their roles in home relationships, forget about health problems, or ignore the needs of their children when they walk through the door at work. Recognizing this, many employers give employees access to an EAP counselor for stress and psychological problems, access to a worksite wellness program to try to address physical problems, and access to some sort of child care vendor to address child care problems. Tying these programs together administratively and calling the package a whole-person, integrated approach barely scratches the surface of what is possible.

Whole-person philosophy goes beyond simply acknowledging the existence of many domains in a person's life, to recognizing the *interactions* between domains. In LWC's whole-person approach, assessment of an employee's situation may uncover spillover effects in several domains, on top of which may be issues caused by the multiple effects together. For example, an employee who is also a parent will worry when his child is sick, and may take time off to care for the child. Between the slowdown from worrying and his time away from work, he falls behind. Stress and a sense of powerlessness give way to burnout and depression. A child care referral program can perhaps help him find assistance with caring for his child. A work-life program may help him explore telecommuting possibilities. Employee assistance can work with him on depression.

A whole-person approach, however, will look for other things also. What's happening physically, and what risks may be involved? Are there mid-life developmental issues? How are these events affecting how he sees himself? The follow-up question is, "Why?"

These different domain areas roughly correspond to different specialty fields (e.g., EAP, wellness). Addressing the domain interactions programmatically produces ongoing multidisciplinary discussions among service staff. Conducted well, these discussions foster cross-discipline understanding, mutual trust, and creativity with collaboration in providing service. An integrated program should produce *synergy*.

Synergy

If a whole-person view of human beings is the primary driving force behind an integrated service format, then synergy should be one of its distinguishing features. Synergy is usually defined by the phrase, "the whole is greater than the sum of its parts." (LWC has adopted the unofficial motto, "The whole person working is better than just some of their parts.") Bringing program pieces together under one roof, physically and/or administratively, is one matter; integrating them operationally is quite another. Programs where EAP, wellness, and work-life are connected administratively, but function independently, are not truly integrated. Synergy is created when staff with different but related domain expertise come together with the common purpose of exploring and creating new services or programs. It spills over into service offerings that provide more broad-based knowledge, are often unique, and have a tighter, better fit to equip employees to manage their real-world life and work situations.

Differentiation and Resiliency

As mentioned previously, systems theory addresses the interactions between an individual and the system(s) of which he is a part. Figure 1 illustrates the case of an individual as part of two systems, symbolized by springs. When one person acts in a way that affects the group, it can be pictured as reverberations that move around the system. Given the characteristics, personalities, context, etc., of the different people in the system, the group will develop unique patterns in the way that they vibrate together. These patterns have a single purpose: to return the system to the stability of its previous state or structure. This characteristic is called homeostasis.

"Differentiation," a concept developed by Murray Bowen (Kerr & Bowen, 1988) and built upon by David Schnarch (Schnarch, 1997), works against homeostasis. Differentiation is the degree to which an

FIGURE 1. An Individual as Part of Two Systems

individual can resist a system's pressure to make him vibrate in the old pattern, back to homeostasis. In relational terms, a highly differentiated individual determines his own role, identity, and behavior independent of the group rather than allowing the group to dictate these factors. A well-differentiated person is able to maintain a sense of self-identity and self-directedness without overwhelming or withdrawing from the larger group.

Differentiation is also a developmental concept, which means that resisting the system's strongest pressures to conform is a natural challenge for the individual to grow up to the next level of differentiation. This requires that the person develop more effective self-soothing and self-validating skills in order to hold his or her ground.

Resiliency is closely related to differentiation and is a quality that increases as differentiation develops. It is, in part, the ability to bounce back, survive, grow, and even thrive in adverse circumstances. Other traits include playful curiosity (Siebert, 1996; also see www.resiliencycenter.com). While differentiation is about a person's ability to maintain self-directedness and self-identity in a system, resiliency provides the self-motivation and efficacy to make the person able to "stay the course" while increasing his or her differentiation. Being a developmental concept also means that employee problems are framed in a positive growth perspective, instead of the negativity of "pathology."

Life-Cycle/Work-Cycle

As life brings circumstances that challenge people to increase their differentiation, it often does so in somewhat predictable ways. Transitional events such as marriage, parenthood, and mid-life reevaluation help define a common "life-cycle." In a sense, the life-cycle concept is akin to "leverage points": There are times and events in life that have a disproportionately greater power to challenge people to differentiate to a higher level. Consequently, focusing program offerings on these common times and events promotes broader utilization and optimal use of resources.

Note that most life-cycle events transcend work, even though they can create spillover at work. In contrast, work-cycle events–a subset of life-cycle events in LWC's philosophy, are those that are defined within work. Promotions, job changes, layoffs, pre-retirement and post-retirement adjustments are examples of work-cycle challenges. Just as life-cycle events can create spillover at work, so also can work-cycle events. Operating in the work environment makes integrated programs like

LWC especially well-equipped to identify, understand, and assist employees facing these challenges.

Because life-cycle and work-cycle events are generally common life experiences, employee assistance, wellness and work-life programs can anticipate them and prepare services for assisting employees.

LWC'S ADAPTATIONS

UA Life & Work Connections' mission is to build resiliency in the individual and in the organization. Employees are seen as assets that should be able to flourish as much as possible, instead of budget lines whose compensation is a "cost of doing business." Building and maintaining resilient employees leads to a much healthier, stronger organization (Hope & Hope, 1997).

Applying the terms, "systemic," "whole-person," "synergy," "differentiation" and "resiliency," and "life-cycle/work-cycle," as defined above, to this mission leads to two guidelines for assessment and intervention. First, the issues that bring a client in for help generally contain some embedded developmental challenge for that employee. More than just problem solving, the goal is to facilitate a developmental process that helps the employee not only resolve the problem at hand, but better equips him to manage future issues. Growth eases the grip that past stressors have had on him.

The second guideline is that building resiliency leads to longer lasting behavioral change. Self-efficacy and self-motivation are core elements in resiliency, and when they are the basis for an employee making changes in his life, the changes tend to "stick" and are longer lasting. Drawing on an employee's intrinsic motivation is more powerful than trying extrinsically, or externally, to motivate him.

STRATEGIC AND TACTICAL SERVICES

Recall that a systemic view considers both the individual as well as his environment, which is the group of systems around him. LWC's efforts to build resiliency in the organization (the employee's work environment) take the form of "strategic" services. Departmental consultations, presentations, classes, and committee involvement are examples of these. LWC's services to individual employees (i.e., counseling, consultations, etc.)

are considered "tactical" services, because they involve the individual "battles" that employees face, which are only a small part in shaping the whole picture.

PUTTING IT ALL TOGETHER

Figure 2 is a depiction of UA Life &Work Connections' model. From left, LWC, composed of its integrated components, with its mission, goals, contract, and partnerships, markets itself and offers strategic services to the University of Arizona workplace, where the individual employees and the institution interact. The combination of unique, individual employees and organizational factors creates a certain level of functioning.

When the level of functioning in a particular workplace drops below a certain threshold (i.e., negative spillover within the unit reaches some subjective level of critical mass), the individual(s) and/or supervisor(s) involved may request specific tactical services from LWC. With the integration of five areas of service and the availability of partnerships to assist, LWC can provide a tailored set of services to meet the need, including referrals as appropriate. These services lead to one or more outcomes, which are intended to increase the individual's resiliency while at the same time increasing the organization's productivity. Regular

FIGURE 2. UA Life and Work Connections' Model

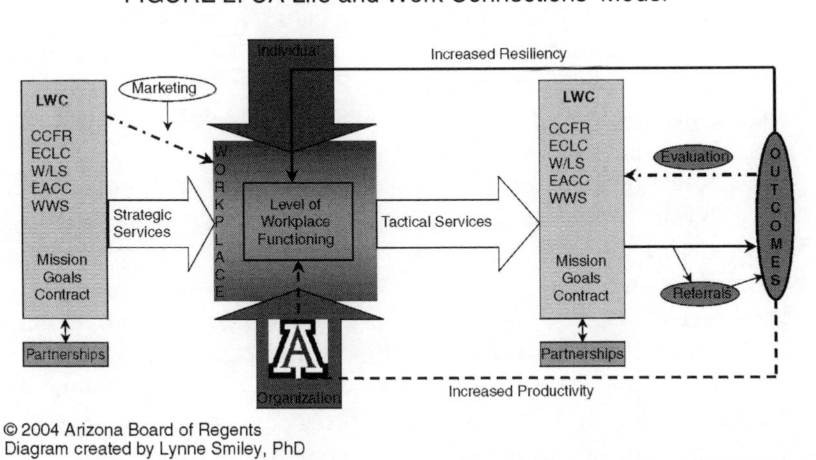

Diagram created by Lynne Smiley, PhD

evaluations help LWC make certain of its effectiveness and reveal any gaps missed in the service.

CASE VIGNETTE

One of LWC's more popular and visible services is the Worksite Wellness Heart Health Screening, usually conducted in the participants' workplace. The screening offers participants an opportunity to have their blood pressure taken, total cholesterol (TC), HDL cholesterol, the ratio of TC to HDL, long-term blood glucose level, weight, body fat percentage, and a perceived exertion exercise recovery test. At the next station in the screening, participants meet with a fitness and nutrition expert on LWC's staff, where their test results are explained in detail, their responses to a fitness and nutrition questionnaire are discussed, and recommendations are made. Finally, participants meet with an employee assistance counselor, who discusses with them their responses on a questionnaire about sleep and stress.

The counselor is an integrated part of the screenings for several reasons. First, it provides exposure to employee assistance services in an upbeat, non-stigmatizing setting. Meeting and getting acquainted with the counselor eliminates one of the barriers to those who may not otherwise seek help. Another reason is the whole-person approach. Employees who are struggling with weight gain in spite of their best efforts to manage it are often also experiencing excessive stress, depression, or other conditions. In many of these cases, eating habits are a minor issue compared to what else may be going on in the client's life. Having a more comprehensive picture can provide more effective strategies to build resiliency. If an employee so chooses to seek help, it now has a name, a face, and a personal connection.

Yet another reason to include employee assistance in the health screening is exposure to EAP as a supervisory resource. For example, some employees in a department that was being screened chose to reveal to each other their (confidential) blood pressure readings, and expressed surprise that many of them were high. As the group talked more, including the supervisor, it dawned on them that there may be a common denominator for the surprise readings. This generated conversation about the work environment, and with EAP assistance, the supervisor and employees began making adjustments to help relieve department-wide stress.

ADVANTAGES OF LWC'S INTEGRATED MODEL

The mission of building resiliency is the means of maximizing productivity and minimizing health care costs in LWC's systemic, whole-person, life-cycle approach. It is designed to be as comprehensive as possible, as a promotion-prevention-intervention-post-intervention model. Along each of the three dimensions (systemic, whole-person, life-cycle) lie a range of possibilities, which, singly, and in combination with each other, affect productivity and health care costs. LWC's model has some advantages:

- *The Capability to Identify a Broader Range of Risk Factors*. The more risk factors an employee has, the greater his overall probability of experiencing a spillover condition. By identifying more of these risk factors to an employee, they can be reduced by preventive education and/or effective intervention.
- *Future Scanning*. The systemic, whole-person, life-cycle nature of LWC's approach allows a broader awareness of new developments, trends, and research (e.g., paucity of skilled workers, rise of depression impact). Through this awareness, LWC can anticipate some shifts and prepare service offerings guided by relevant research.
- *Lower Overhead and Administration*. Because it is an internal model housed under one roof, LWC does not have to negotiate with other vendors and the client. The five components of LWC answer to a single administrator (the director), who makes the necessary networking contacts.
- *Flexibility and Collaboration*. Service offerings can be creatively combined to meet the unique needs of a particular client or group. There are also occasions where any of several LWC staff can cover one type of presentation leading to quicker response times.
- *Synergy*. Frequent informal and lively discussions occur among staff about some research topic or societal trend. Mutual respect and trust develop. These interactions not only keep the team members sharp and in touch, but they also provide opportunities to brainstorm and think "outside the box."
- *Reduced Costs*. Having a broad, multidisciplinary base, the model is designed so that losses of productivity and health care costs increases are minimized.
- *Enhances Risk Management*. In January 2004, the Arizona Board of Regents released an audit of the University of Arizona's Loss

Prevention Program. The UA Life & Work Connections program was specifically cited as a positive benefit to the UA and its employees through ". . . reduced loss of life, hours, and property through substance abuse training for supervisors; reduced absenteeism, illness and employee recruitment costs through teaching of stress management and assisting employees with stress reduction."

CHALLENGES TO THE INTEGRATED MODEL

- *Metrics.* Establishing reliable metrics is difficult due to the difficulty in establishing outcome definitions, measuring prevention, and overcoming privacy issues. There is also the added difficulty of measuring how integrated services are more effective than "silo" approaches.
- *Personnel.* Much of the value of synergy and integration will be lost if the staff refuses to cooperate with each other. Beyond effectively resolving conflict, synergy will be compromised when there is not a general sense of being part of the team. Playful curiosity, and the ability to learn quickly and be mentally and emotionally flexible are critical to success of each individual and the integrated team as a whole (Siebert, 1996; also see www.resiliencycenter.com).

DETAILED CASE APPLICATION

The following true story is presented in detail to illustrate the complexity of the many systems and groups of people affected by tragic events that recently occurred at the university, and to demonstrate how integration made LWC's response to these events effective.

The Events

On the clear, chilly Monday morning of October 28, 2002, fourth semester nursing student Robert Flores walked into the College of Nursing building on the University of Arizona campus with five guns and 150 rounds of ammunition in his backpack. Several individuals recalled saying "Hi" to him as he passed by. He went first into the 2nd floor office of Robin Rogers, a nursing instructor who taught his class the previous semester, closed the door, and shot her twice, killing her. Flores then proceeded upstairs to the 4th floor, where the class he was currently enrolled in was taking a test. He walked into the room, asked Cheryl

McGaffic, one of the course's two instructors, if she was ready to meet her Maker, and when she replied, "Yes," he shot her several times at pointblank range, killing her. The 46 students in the class screamed and dove for cover behind desks, tables, chairs, whatever they could find. Flores then curtly dismissed them from the classroom. After a moment's fearful hesitation, they rushed to the doors to get out. When the room cleared, he shot and killed Barbara Monroe, the other course instructor, before finally turning the gun on himself.

One of the fleeing students, not knowing that Flores was dead, ran into a nearby office and told the occupants to call 911. As word spread through the building, many chose to run while others locked themselves in their offices. By amazing coincidence, a Tucson Police Department SWAT team was at a nearby park, already geared up for a training exercise. They were at the College of Nursing in seven minutes and began a floor-by-floor search for potentially several gunmen (with the dead on two different floors, some concluded that there was more than one gunman). Those who had locked themselves in offices were afraid to open their doors. The pounding, shouting people in the hallways, who were demanding they unlock the doors, could be the police (who had no keys) or gunmen. When doors were not opened, the SWAT team blew them open and stormed the room. Terrified occupants were told to get out of the building as quickly as they could. By ones and twos they ran out, huddling together in small groups in the parking lot.

In other nearby buildings on the Arizona Health Sciences Center campus, including University Medical Center hospital, occupants received diverse and often conflicting instructions about what they should do. Some ended up needlessly enduring an anxiety-filled six-hour wait in their darkened, locked offices before someone remembered to inform them that the danger was over.

The media, of course, immediately picked up on the event, and were on scene almost as quickly as the SWAT team. Local television stations cut into regular programming and carried live reports from the scene, becoming the first source of information for many in the campus community, including family members of students, faculty, and staff.

Flores' final act of defiant revenge was a 22-page letter that he had written and mailed to a local newspaper before the shootings, timed to be received the day after the shootings. The paper printed part of the letter but posted its entirety online. The letter was a long, rambling recital of perceived wrongs that had been inflicted on him, which he used to justify the killings. The letter sparked a good deal of anger and only added to the follow-up work for LWC.

THE RESPONSE

Many people and different units on campus got involved to assist students and employees in the immediate aftermath. LWC led the recovery effort because of its ability to work with individuals as well as layers of organizational systems. Systemically, progress on both sides is intertwined, and therefore the best recovery outcomes required working on both sides simultaneously. Other campus units collaborated with LWC, including Risk Management, Campus Health Services, CAPS, the student counseling center, and Human Resources. Those people who had been closest to the shootings–several hundred people–were herded into a nearby building away from the media. A systemic approach was used so that the eyewitnesses (the "hot" group) were separated from the rest (the "warm" group) and moved to a separate room; Critical Incident Stress Management ("CISM") interventions were begun for both groups. In the coming days and weeks, there would also be interventions for groups in other health sciences colleges, in a number of other specific departments on the main campus, and two "Town Hall" meetings for the entire campus community.

LWC's integrated response began with the worksite wellness coordinator assisting the organizing efforts at the request of employee assistance. By mid-morning planning discussions were taking place with upper administration from the Arizona Health Sciences Center and from the university proper. During these discussions, the worksite wellness coordinator called attention to the fact that the physiological effects of traumatic stress were soon going to put people in urgent need of sustenance. Food, drinks and water were ordered immediately.

Integration led to other contributions and task assignments. LWC's administrative associate became a "gopher," taking care of rescheduling clients and arranging for materials, rooms, and other needs. The Human Resource Specialist working in the child care component shifted her duties to cover the phones, while the child care component coordinator pulled together and posted guidelines for families about responding to children's fear and questions on its Web site.

Calls from external CISM vendors offering their services began pouring in and had to be assessed. College of Nursing and university administrators needed assistance from someone familiar with trauma to make decisions about next steps: How long a wait is appropriate until resuming classes? How should faculty be involved in making these decisions? What kind of memorial service would be appropriate and helpful for grieving people? What should be done about the victims' offices and the classroom where the murders took place? How are these decisions made when the decision makers themselves are in shock and grief?

In response, LWC began providing ongoing consultations to work with administrators both as humans responding to a traumatic event and as professionals struggling to make business recovery decisions. These consultations, which addressed workgroup dynamics, reclaiming the working and learning environment, student responses and concerns, and more, continued throughout the following year.

LWC decided to partner with a volunteer CISM network sponsored by the Northwest Fire and Rescue District. The volunteers were made up of firefighters, hospital, and ER nurses, and school counselors who were all trained and experienced with CISM. Sixteen volunteers showed up the next day, some coming from nearly 200 miles away.

The integrated response and partnerships with Northwest Fire and Rescue District's CISM team and other campus groups led to three remarkable outcomes. First, every one of the students who witnessed the murder of their teacher graduated on time, having passed the full curriculum requirements. Second, not one employee of the College of Nursing resigned because of the shootings. On the contrary, over the following year, some fifteen new faculty were added without questioning the security of the college. Finally, as of this writing two years after the shootings, there have been no lawsuits against the university stemming from the shootings.

This scenario, and a handful of others like it, represents an extreme in the intensity and scale of problems encountered by LWC. They are not the norm of everyday functioning. The bulk of the work takes the form of small day-to-day breakthroughs; an employee learning to say "no" and set better boundaries, another learning to have a hard conversation with an aging parent, and another learning self-care regarding diabetes.

CONCLUSIONS

Recognizing that spillover has many sources and takes many forms, integration, as LWC has defined it, was a strategic innovation to address employees as whole people. The strategy of integration is intended to develop whole-person resiliency.

This is a very critical time for EAPs, wellness and work-life programs. In today's context of depleted budgets, a shrinking force of skilled workers, and skyrocketing health care costs, employee assistance, wellness and work-life services must fully realize their value and innovatively step forward. A mountain of research has been piling up, demonstrating, in terms of dollars lost, just how shockingly costly spillover is–likely in the tens of millions of dollars for an institution like the University of Arizona (Goetzel, 2003; Kessler, 2001). The development of accurate, *meaningful* metrics is crucial in order to connect outcomes with dollars saved; demonstrating how integrated programs contribute in terms of reducing health care costs, productivity costs, and meeting recruitment and retention goals.

> Not everything that matters can be measured, and not everything that can be measured matters.
>
> –Einstein

REFERENCES

Goetzel, R. Z. et al. (2003). The Health and Productivity Cost Burden of the "Top 10" Physical and Mental Health Conditions Affecting Six Large US Employers in 1999. *Journal of Occupational and Environmental Medicine,* 45:5-14.

Gryzwacz, J. (2000). Work-Family Spillover and Health During Midlife: Is Managing Conflict Everything? *American Journal of Health Promotion*, 14:236-243.

Grzywacz, J. & Fuqua, J. (1999). The Social Ecology of Health: Leverage Points and Linkages. *Behavioral Medicine,* 26:3.

Grzywacz, J. & Marks, N. (2000). Reconceptualizing the Work-Family Interface: An Ecological Perspective on the Correlates of Positive and Negative Spillover Between Work and Family. *Journal of Occupational Health Psychology,* 5:1, 111-126.

Hope, J. & Hope, T. (1997). *Competing in the Third Wave.* Boston: Harvard Business School Press.

Kerr, M. & Bowen, M. (1988). *Family Evaluation: An Approach Based on Bowen Theory.* New York: W.W. Norton.

Kessler, R. C. et al. (2001). The Effects of Chronic Medical Conditions on Work Loss and Cutback. *Journal of Occupational and Environmental Medicine,* 43:218-225.

Office of Decision Planning and Support, University of Arizona (2004). "The University of Arizona FAQ, 2003-2004" Brochure.

Schnarch, D. (1997). *Passionate Marriage.* NY: Henry Holt and Co.

Siebert, A. (1996). *Survivor Personality.* NY: Ley Publications.

Siebert, A. (2004). The Resiliency Center Web site. www.resiliencycenter.com.

Swihart, D. L. & Thompson, D. A. (2002). Successful Program Integration: An Analysis of the Challenges and Opportunities Facing an EAP That Integrated with Other Programs Reveals the Keys to Successfully Serving the Systemic Needs of Employees and Work Organizations. *EAP Association Exchange, 32*(5): 10-13.

doi:10.1300/J490v22n03_10

Responding to Deaths of Faculty, Staff and Students at UC, Berkeley–An Integrated Approach

Carol Hoffman
Bruce Goya

SUMMARY. This article describes an important initiative designed to address the deaths of faculty, staff, and students at the University of California at Berkeley. Work-life and EAP practitioners can play a significant role in reducing the distress and lost work time associated with workplace deaths by helping employers to plan a response to employee and client deaths, and by participating in implementing that response. A model framework is presented to demonstrate the vital need for coordination and integration among many of the employers' programs, services, and activities in order to address deaths. doi:10.1300/J490v22n03_11

KEYWORDS. Death, grief, employer response to death, workplace death, program evaluation matrix, work culture evaluation, workplace integration, program integration, program evaluation measures

[Haworth co-indexing entry note]: "Responding to Deaths of Faculty, Staff and Students at UC, Berkeley–An Integrated Approach." Hoffman, Carol and Bruce Goya. Co-published simultaneously in *Journal of Workplace Behavioral Health* (The Haworth Press, Inc.) Vol. 22, No. 2/3, 2006/2007, pp. 161-175; and: *Employee Assistance Programs in Higher Education* (ed: R. Paul Maiden and Sally B. Philips) The Haworth Press, 2006/2007, pp. 161-175. Single or multiple copies of this article are available for a fee from The Haworth Document Delivery Service [1-800-HAWORTH, 9:00 a.m. - 5:00 p.m. (EST). E-mail address: docdelivery@haworthpress.com].

Available online at http://jwbh.haworthpress.com

doi:10.1300/J490v22n03_11

AN INTEGRATED APPROACH TO DEATH IN THE ACADEMIC SETTING

Many working people may experience at least one death of someone they know during their working lives. This someone could be a coworker who died on site at the workplace or from an accident or illness away from the workplace. The deceased could also be a client or customer of the workplace or known to employees through some work-related activity.

Work-life and EAP practitioners can play a significant role in helping to reduce the distress and lost work time associated with workplace deaths by assisting to plan a response to employee and client deaths, and by participating in implementing that response. This article will demonstrate the vital need for coordination and integration among many employer programs, services, and activities, including work-life and EAP, using the University of California at Berkeley as a model.

DEATH IN THE WORKPLACE

The time following a death of someone whose life was spent in the workplace, or as a significant client of the workplace, can be of critical importance. Having a clear plan involving the necessary departments and outlining key roles and expectations can assure that the response to the death is comprehensive and effective, comforting those adjusting to the loss and attending to issues both personal and practical.

Establishing the anticipated death rate for employees and customers or clients ("clients" will be used in this article to indicate both) can help employers to prepare for this inevitable life cycle event. To estimate the number of deaths per year in your workplace, simply apply the death rate of the appropriate demographic group in the general population (available through census data) to your population of employees and clients.

In the university setting the faculty and staff are the employees, the students are the clients, and all are integral to the workplace community. A death of a faculty, staff, or student can have a far-reaching impact on other members of that community. Nationally, many factors contribute to the importance of examining the way in which deaths and bereavement are handled in the workplace, including:

- Increasing diversity of the population, with varying views, beliefs, and practices regarding death.

- Increased use of guns, resulting in more sudden, violent deaths.
- Greater awareness of the causes of deaths, such as alcohol and drugs, eating disorders, domestic violence, smoking, and other conditions that make it more difficult to minimize and cover up how colleagues and families die.
- More chronic, life-threatening illnesses such as cancer and AIDS that can be treated medically, allowing the affected individual to continue participating in the workplace, sometimes up until the day they die.
- Location of the workplace in a region with natural disasters such as earthquakes, fires, floods, and mudslides.
- Deaths occurring geographically far from the workplace, as employees work and vacation in other parts of the nation and the world.
- Increasing numbers of elderly relatives of employees, sometimes with chronic and terminal conditions, who die after years of caregiving by the employee.
- More immediate awareness of the deaths of colleagues and family members who live and work far away from the workplace due to increased communication technologies.
- Terrorism, war, and violence, which can affect any worksite, locally or internationally, at any time.

INTEGRATION OF EAP AND WORK-LIFE WITH OTHER PROGRAMS

Comprised of approximately 15,000 employees and 35,000 students, University of California (UC)-Berkeley is one of the largest employers in the east bay area, across the bridge from San Francisco. UC Berkeley's EAP and work-life programs are organizationally situated in the University Health Services, which provides primary medical and mental health care to students as well as health and wellness programs for faculty and staff. Along with employee assistance and work-life programs, the University Health Services faculty/staff programs consist of wellness, ergonomics, vocational rehabilitation, workers' compensation, disability management, and occupational health services for UC Berkeley employees.

Each of these programs operates independently, with a program manager reporting to the assistant vice chancellor, University Health and Counseling Services. Program planning and development are coordinated by a team comprised of the managers of each program. While intake for each program and its components is separate, publicity for workshops, brown bag presentations, and other activities are integrated. This model of separated but coordinated services is designed to preserve the integrity of each program, promote trust in the confidentiality of the EAP, increase awareness and support for all programs, and avoid both overlaps and gaps in services.

UC Berkeley experiences about 20 faculty and staff deaths each year. In addition, there are approximately 10 students and over 100 emeriti/retiree deaths.[1] As many as thirty to fifty different units or departments may be involved in responding to a single death at UC Berkeley.

To address this, in 1999 the Chancellor sponsored a major effort to develop death response guidelines for employees and other members of the university community. Before the guidelines were established, each time a UC Berkeley employee died the supervisor or manager would call many departments in the workplace to seek guidance on what to do and how to do it. The need to continually reinvent a death response protocol led to great waste and inefficiency, as well as unnecessary discomfort for all involved. Moreover, discrepancies in the response to each death often left survivors feeling hurt and disrespected.

The first step towards developing the university's new Guidelines for Responding to Death was to identify gaps and duplications in the response process. Now, employees can turn to the Guidelines for a single, reliable reference that assures greater ease and consistency in responding to campus deaths.

BEYOND EAP AND WORK-LIFE

Both EAPs and work-life programs may be called on to address issues related to a death. Employee assistance programs typically are charged with addressing the emotional aftermath of death. Work-life programs focus on life-cycle issues that impinge on work, from birth to death, though most work-life programs have not yet embraced death as an issue in their purview.[2] It is easy to see how these two programs could benefit from a coordinated, integrated approach to dealing with a campus death. But integration can go much further.

While these two programs are important cogs in the wheel, a successful response to a campus death will involve numerous roles and departments. UC Berkeley has developed a collaborative approach to campus deaths that doesn't stop with EAP and work-life programs. By taking a broader approach, UC Berkeley has been effective and efficient in its responses, simultaneously benefiting the university and the bereaved. Gaps and duplication of efforts have been reduced or eliminated, families are relieved of multiple requests for the same information, and the bereaved no longer receive an impersonal form letter following a loss. Some of the many departments involved in the university's integrated death response include benefits, human resources, payroll, information systems and technology, library, public affairs, and parking and transportation.

Integration of death response services is also an issue in non-academic settings. In any workplace, a death is likely to touch many individuals and affect diverse functions beyond those that will be addressed by EAP and work-life programs. Below is a Program Integration Model that visually demonstrates how program integration can improve overall program effectiveness. Here the model is applied to the death of a member of the campus community.

THE PROGRAM INTEGRATION MODEL

The University of California (UC) environment is decentralized and diverse, with ten campuses (one being UC Berkeley), three national laboratories, and five medical centers. Although they share most policies and benefits, each setting has a somewhat different array of services and programs and its own organizational culture. The Program Integration Model developed at UC is part of an effort to bring order to a sometimes chaotic system of responsibilities and services. It helps by creating an integrated, effective model to facilitate the discussion at UC among various programs such as employee assistance, work-life, vocational rehabilitation, workers' compensation, human resources, and benefits. The model provides a useful structure for plotting the collaboration among multiple entities addressing events in the life of an employee or client that have ramifications for the workplace.

In *Integral Psychology*, Ken Wilber (2001) posits the value of a matrix comparing individual and societal concerns with subjective and objective measures. His framework was adapted to help identify a broader context in which to assess program integration across campuses within UC and across departments within the campus. While Wilber uses the matrix to demonstrate the integration of an individual within a larger universe, the Program Integration Model[3] is an adaptation that demonstrates individual and program integration within the workplace, or in this instance, the University.

The Program Integration Model offers a means of organizing programs and activities within four major categories or quadrants. This model has broad utility for individual program planning and evaluation, or to establish an employer profile of employee-related programs. Plotting programs in the four quadrants highlights the importance of balanced program planning in addressing the needs of both the employee and the employer.

By plotting its programs within the proposed quadrants, an organization will develop a profile that can serve as a road map for improving its balance and addressing programmatic needs at all levels. For example, comprehensive work-life efforts should address the need for leadership support to affect the corporate culture, help with HR policy and benefit design, and include programs such as employee assistance programs to support individuals and families. A complete picture of work-life initiatives within the model will identify gaps and opportunities for future program planning. By plotting program components into the quadrants, an organization can begin to identify individual program strengths and weaknesses, leading toward strategies for improvement.

The premise for this model is that both subjective and objective measures are important to assess program effectiveness for an individual or an organization. While all organizations and programs impact all four quadrants, not all program development intentionally includes in its planning the desire to effectively impact all quadrant areas. For example, the only credible way of measuring a human resources program's "return on investment (ROI)" is to measure its objective elements. However, it has always been difficult to measure the importance, objectively, of employee values, morale and psychological well-being. Therefore, the model distinguishes between subjective and objective programs or program components and also distinguishes between individual and group attributes.

Subjective programs identify and measure values. Objective programs measure specific, identifiable outcomes. For example, when an employer establishes for itself "Principles of Community"[4] initiatives the measure of impact upon the workplace is subjective and difficult to assess, whereas the success of an on-site child care program may be more easily assessed through objective measures. Each company will have different quadrant profiles, and while programs within two different companies may have the same name (e.g., work-life), their program quadrant profiles are likely to be very different.

Using separate descriptive categories of "corporate" and "individual" to intersect "subjective" and "objective" value measures, the resulting grid allows for an assessment of program integration within the work environment. As illustrated in Figure 1, this model serves as an effective program planning and analysis tool.

The first two quadrants of the model focus on issues from the organization's perspective. *Quadrant #1* (Figure 2) focuses on the *organization's culture* and how that culture impacts those working within the organization.

Quadrant #2 (Figure 3) focuses on the *organization's infrastructure.* It represents the framework that supports the workforce and the culture of the organization.

Clearly drawing a hard line between Quadrants 1 and 2 is artificial. Indeed, some of the organization's infrastructure results from its culture. For example, academic cultural values very much affect the development

FIGURE 1. Program Integration Model

Quadrant #1: ***Corporate Subjective***	**Quadrant #2:** ***Corporate Objective***
• Organizational culture • Cultural values • Corporate vision statement	• Organizational infrastructure • Systems • Product lines
Quadrant #3: ***Individual Subjective***	**Quadrant #4:** ***Individual Objective***
• Individual psychological well-being • Individual values	• Individual physical well-being • Individual work

FIGURE 2. Quadrant #1: Organizational Subjective Measures

This quadrant includes statements and values that identify the organization's world view and defines the context and values of the organization. The culture's communal values, shared language, and perceptions are all plotted in this quadrant. In the UC culture, this quadrant holds the shared values of academic excellence, research, teaching, collegiality, and public service.

An organization's culture is a subjective measure. Every organization has a culture that influences how the work gets done and how the organization relates to its employees. The culture represents communal values, shared perceptions, and meanings. This quadrant defines the background context and values of an organization as well as the overall employee morale. In many instances a company's vision statement will reflect the company's cultural values.

of administrative protocol within the University. Likewise, some infrastructure decisions are made for the express purpose of effecting changes in the organization's culture. For example, the early affirmative action plan was established within the University to facilitate the development of a workplace culture more accepting of diversity within the workforce. The third and fourth quadrants are focused at the individual level, identifying program characteristics related to individual values and activities, as well as the individual's response to the organizational culture and administrative systems.

Quadrant #3 (Figure 4) focuses on an employee's *individual psychological well-being, values, and morale* as they affect job performance.

Quadrant #4 (Figure 5) focuses on the employee's *individual physical well-being and productive capability.*

Historically, it appears that most employers have focused their efforts on improving quadrants 2 and 4, representing corporate and individual programs that may be objectively measured. As a result, there is an effort to measure subjective programs and initiatives solely by objective measures which often fail to capture their impact on the workplace. Measuring an employee assistance program by the number of employees seen, for example, would miss the point of the program. Work-life program elements that are selected to support a "return on investment"

FIGURE 3. Quadrant #2: Organizational Objective Measures

This quadrant identifies an organization's infrastructure, systems, and product lines. An organization's infrastructure includes all corporate programs that are objectively measured. At the University, this infrastructure includes finance administration, personnel policies, labor relations, insurance benefits, the physical plant, and systems (information technology).

FIGURE 4. Quadrant #3: Individual Subjective Measures

This quadrant includes the individual's sense of self, well-being, and values. Individual morale may dictate the level of engagement in work and productivity. At the university, programs impacting this quadrant might include stress reduction seminars, conflict resolution, and employee assistance programs.

FIGURE 5. Quadrant #4: Individual Objective Measures

This quadrant includes programs such as nutrition classes, disease management, on-site medical services, and wellness programs. Examples related to productivity may include employee training programs, ergonomic workstations, and work tools.

are different from those that are concerned with the subjective climate of the organization, even though both ultimately influence productivity.

Plotting workplace or program components within the quadrants makes us acutely aware of the ways in which all aspects of work–culture, infrastructure, and psychological and physical well-being–affect, and are affected by each other. To be effective, a comprehensive program must address not only its own area of purview, but must coordinate with other programs, and if located primarily within one quadrant area, coordinate with programs in the other quadrants.

Plotting the University's EAP and work-life programs components identified within the quadrants of the Program Integration Model revealed interesting inter-program working relationships.

- First, it was noticed that most UC EAP and work-life programs emphasized program activities in one quadrant rather than in all four quadrants. For instance, one UC campus' work-life program focused on developing program initiatives that would be identified within Quadrant 2 whereas another work-life program focused more on organizational culture (Quadrant 1). It was discovered that most EAP activities within UC would be located within Quadrant 3 and most work-life activities would be located in Quadrant 2. Quadrant 2 activities may include coordinating/providing child care support, lactation support, and HR policy coordination supporting work-life initiatives.
- Second, viewing the programs plotted into the quadrants helped to make it clear why there has been historic difficulty in making comparisons among programs across the UC campuses and medical centers–most programs initially attempt to address specific campus issues rather than to achieve balance among the four quadrants.
- Finally, it was noticed in plotting the university's diverse programs, there were many that, while not traditionally defined as work-life or employee assistance programs, had an important impact on an employee's work and life relationships, and psychological health. The model reinforced the need for better integration of EAP and work-life programs with other departments such as human resources, safety, benefits, risk, and legal.

It is within this context that the UC Berkeley initiative on responding to death is now reviewed. This initiative is an example of a program developed to address the concerns identified across all four of the model's quadrants. Plotting the program components has helped to identify program strengths and weaknesses, and has provided a road map for future strategic program planning.

RESPONDING TO A DEATH AT UC BERKELEY

In order to comprehensively address employee issues, work-life programs address life issues from cradle to grave. Yet many organizations have no process in place for responding to an employee death. Some employers may not recognize the need for such a program, while others may be uncomfortable planning for this difficult life transition.

An inadequate or absent response to an employee death can weaken or break the ties of trust and loyalty that enable other employees to remain engaged and productive in their work. Employees may not remember all of the baby showers, birthdays, and other life events of coworkers, but they can relay as if it were yesterday what the employer did or did not do when someone died. The response to death does not seem to leave the institutional memory.[5]

In order to improve its response to campus deaths, in 1999 UC Berkeley began developing a nationally recognized program that includes guidelines, a Website, a virtual memorial, and an annual memorial event. The program's target audience includes faculty and staff, students, emeriti, and retirees.

The objective of the UC Berkeley death-response program is to build a sense of community by addressing the most difficult of life events: the death of a member of the campus community. The program supports the community by simultaneously addressing the needs of the organization and of its employees. Responding to deaths effectively and compassionately assures more efficient operations while addressing the emotional needs and functioning of staff and faculty. The employer may benefit by greater loyalty, increased retention, improved productivity, and enhanced morale.

UC Berkeley's death-response program helps employees navigate a host of campus death-related benefits, policies and programs, including family sick leave, bereavement leave, personal leave, catastrophic leave-sharing, flexible work arrangements, telecommuting, health benefits, domestic partner benefits, disability benefits, accidental benefits, life insurance, dependent care, employee assistance, emergency loans, long-term care insurance, group legal services, and elder/adult dependent care.

The death-response Website [http://death-response.chance.berkeley.edu] functions as the program's hub. It provides a link to the campus Guidelines for Responding to Death, which offers tools to help the campus respond thoroughly and consistently to the needs of family and colleagues following a death. Because each life and death is unique, individual judgment is always necessary. The guidelines help users respond to those judgment calls.

The Website includes detailed guidance for handling the response to every aspect of a campus member's death, with a step-by-step outline of actions to be taken when a death occurs, including:

- How to choose who will be responsible for coordinating the response to a death and an explanation of that role,
- A timeline with detailed information on communications, condolences, survivors' emotional needs, memorial events, and other issues, and
- A list of specific considerations for each population (students, faculty, staff, emeriti, and retirees).

A feature on the site enables users to automatically e-mail a form with pertinent information to all required parties on campus. The automated e-mail program assures that necessary information gets to the right departments, such as the benefits and human resources offices, in a timely and convenient manner.

Information for members of the campus who have lost loved ones also is available on the Website. This includes what the workplace can do when a family member dies and another section on how to deal with grief and loss. There is also a section on preparing for one's own death; putting financial, legal, and medical documents in order in advance eases the burden on survivors. Campus resources, such as an emergency loan program that can be used for death-related expenses, are also listed.

University visitors to the site may create a virtual memorial–a Web page in memory of a family member, friend, or other, either within or outside of the university. Finally, the program established an annual public memorial event honoring members of the campus community who have died during the previous year. This ceremony gives equal weight to the memory of those who were lost in the past year, no matter what their workplace stature or role during their lifetime. This helps to balance the memorial services offered at the time of death for distinguished faculty (such as Nobel Laureates) with the same recognition for other employees such as custodians.

Created by a Chancellor-appointed work group, Berkeley's progressive program for responding to campus deaths has been recognized nationally. Universities and corporations around the country have inquired about Berkeley's death-response procedures, and the program has been referred to in journals and periodicals.

THE PROGRAM INTEGRATION MODEL AND THE RESPONSE TO DEATH INITIATIVE

The Program Integration Model emphasizes the need for balanced program planning that addresses the needs of both the employer and the employee. Though the model was not used in the development and implementation of the death initiative at UC Berkeley, it can now be used for assessment and review of the current program to evaluate program efficacy. Establishing a model profile of the Response to Death Initiative provides the framework that allows for discussion of programmatic balance, resources, and coordination.

A simple listing of Initiative programs and benefits within the respective quadrants of the model creates an "Initiative" profile. The completed model (Figure 6) shows all the programs and benefits coordinated for an effective response to a death at the Berkeley campus, providing support for survivors, coworkers, and the employer community.

Balance. Programs and benefits assembled together for this Initiative are comprehensive and provide significant effort in each of the quadrants within the model. Individual and work community values are enhanced; employee and survivor resources are identified and readily accessible. In addition to improving a coordinated response to death, UC Berkeley demonstrates that it values a compassionate response to death, further reinforcing work-culture values of honoring people and their ideas, critical for an academic institution.

Coordination. Program and benefit coordination with the identified goal of establishing an effective and coordinated response to death allows each program to participate in identifying a process and role in supporting the desired outcome.

Effectiveness. Improving program effectiveness by supporting a comprehensive and coordinated response to death in the workplace is the goal. Codifying identified process improvements (see *http://death-reponse.* chance.berkeley.edu) creates a new base upon which future improvements may be made. Periodic process evaluations including placing programs

FIGURE 6. Model Profile of UC Berkeley's Response to Death Initiative

Quadrant #1: ***Organizational Subjective***	**Quadrant #2:** ***Organizational Objective***
• Community memorials • Condolences • Obituaries • Diversity	• Group life insurance • AD&D benefits • Survivor benefits • Emergency leaves • Emergency loans • Survivor notification • Inter-program coordination • Integrated Web resource for family members and coworkers
Quadrant #3: ***Individual Subjective***	**Quadrant #4:** ***Individual Objective***
• EAP • Dependent care assistance • Personal leave • Bereavement leave • Family sick • Virtual memorials	• Health benefits • Catastrophic leave sharing • FMLA • Flexible work arrangements

in all quadrants are required to ensure the Initiative continues to be responsive and current.

The UC Berkeley *Response to Death Initiative* is a premier model of effective program coordination that promotes corporate and individual values while delivering enhanced services and improved program efficiencies. Family members, coworkers, managers, and customers all benefit from comprehensive programming in response to this significant life event. From reinforcing a common value within the workplace to the reduction of program duplication and inefficiency, from providing emotional support for coworkers to the efficient delivery of benefits to family members, the *Response to Death Initiative* provides an example of enhancing objective and subjective values within the workplace. A comprehensive, effective and well-integrated response to a significant event, such as death, demonstrates respect for both individuals and the community.

NOTES

1. Anticipated death rates are based on review of census death rates data based on age and numbers of people in each age group at UC Berkeley. (Thank you to Jon Bain-Chekal, MBA, for this data collection and other work on this project.) These estimates have proven correct over the last four years that the data has been collected.

2. The statement that most work-life programs do not address death-related issues is based on the author's informal discussions with university and other industry work-life professionals, the topic areas covered in workshops, etc., at work-life conferences, and a review of work-life literature.

3. This model was developed in 2000 for the University of California by Judy McConnell, Kris Lange, and Bruce Goya. Judy McConnell, Director of Health & Welfare Administration, has since retired from the University. Kris Lange and Bruce Goya work in the Human Resources and Benefits Department at the University of California Office of the President. This Model was presented to the Alliance of Work-Life Progress (AWLP) conference in February 2002.

4. "Principles of Community" provide stated values of community interaction. See the UC San Diego Principles of Community at http://www.ucsd.edu/principles/ for an example.

5. Based on feedback from workshop participants and EAP clients plus observational experience.

doi:10.1300/J490v22n03_11

APPENDICES

Responding to deaths Website, including the virtual memorial, *http://death-response. chance.berkeley.edu*

One article in the employee newspaper about the updated and improved website and memorial event, *http://www.berkeley.edu/news/berkeleyan/2002/09/memorial.html*

Communication to all employees from the Chancellor announcing the Website and memorial event 9/10/04, *http://www.berkeley.edu/news/media/releases/2004/09/ memoriam.* shtml

The Berkeley response to deaths program has been highlighted in:

- HR Magazine, *Giving Time to Grieve,* November 1999, *and Helping Employees Cope with Grief*, September 2003, published by the Society for Human Resource
- Management The Robert Wood Johnson Foundation Last Acts Coalition in their materials on end of life issues.
- One Small Step *Newsteps*, Summer 2003, Vol. 2, No. 3

Wilber, Ken (2000) *Integral Psychology*, Shambhala Publications, Inc. USA

Index

Page numbers followed by a *t*, *f*, or *n* indicate tables, figures, or notes.

For Product Safety Concerns and Information please contact our EU representative GPSR@taylorandfrancis.com Taylor & Francis Verlag GmbH, Kaufingerstraße 24, 80331 München, Germany

Printed and bound by CPI Group (UK) Ltd, Croydon, CR0 4YY
11/04/2025
01843992-0011